Contents

CW00550214

How to use this guide

This guide is divided into two parts:

- **Part 1** Explains what a fire risk assessment is and how you might go about it. Your fire risk assessment should be the foundation for all the fire precautions at your premises.

- **Part 2** Provides further guidance on fire precautions. The information is provided for you and others to dip into when carrying out your fire risk assessment or when you are reviewing your existing fire precautions.

Appendices provide supplementary information.

If any part of your premises is listed as of historic interest, additional information is available in Appendix D.

Note: This guide has primarily been written for protecting from fire all people present at any equine and agricultural establishment. Current and proposed animal legislation, including the Government's equine strategy documents, which refer to the provisions for animal welfare arrangements, also applies to the appropriate arrangements to protect horses and other large animals from fire.

Preface

This guide applies to England and Wales only and is to be used in conjunction with the Regulatory Reform (Fire Safety) Order 2005.

Outside England and Wales, this document may be used as general guidance if no other local guidance is available.

It does not set prescriptive standards, but provides recommendations and guidance for use when assessing the adequacy of fire precautions in stables and all animal premises. Other fire risk assessment methods may be equally valid to comply with fire safety law.

Your existing fire safety arrangements may not be the same as the recommendations used in this guide but, as long as you can demonstrate that they meet an equivalent standard of fire safety, they are likely to be acceptable. If you decide that your existing arrangements are not satisfactory, there may be other ways to comply with fire safety law. This means there is no obligation to adopt any particular solution in this guide if you prefer to meet the requirement in some other way.

Where the buildings have been recently constructed or significantly altered, the fire detection and fire warning arrangements, escape routes and facilities for the fire and rescue service should have been designed, constructed and installed in accordance with current building regulations. In such cases, it is likely that these measures will be satisfactory as long as they are being properly maintained and no significant increase in risk has been introduced.

This guide should not be used to design fire safety in new buildings. Where alterations are proposed to existing stables and animal premises, they may be subject to building regulations. However, it can be used to develop the fire safety strategy for the building.

Introduction

WHO SHOULD USE THIS GUIDE?

This guide is for use at all equine establishments, stables, livery yards and other animal establishments and for all employers, proprietors, managers, occupiers and owners. It tells you what you have to do to comply with fire safety law and it also helps you to carry out a fire risk assessment and identify the general fire precautions you need to have in place.

This guide has been designed so that a responsible person, with no formal training or experience, should be able to carry out a fire risk assessment in smaller, less complicated equine establishments, stables, livery yards, and other animal establishments. If you decide, having read this guide, that you are unable to apply the guidance, then you should seek expert advice. Larger and more complex premises and establishments are likely to need to be assessed by a person who has further training or experience in fire risk assessment.

This guide may also be useful for:

• employees;

• employee-elected representatives;

• trade union-appointed health and safety representatives;

• enforcing authorities;

• insurance assessors; and

• all other people who have a role in ensuring fire safety in equine establishments and similar venues.

This guide applies to premises where the main use of the building(s) or part of the building is as stables or livery yards, or equine establishments forming part of other occupancy premises, e.g. stables at racecourses. It may also be suitable for individual stables within other complexes, such as zoos, large animal sanctuaries or farm parks, although consultation with the occupancy managers will be necessary.

This guide may be used in conjunction with other guides in the series, for instance guide 2 – factories and warehouses, to inform risk assessments in other establishments as appropriate.

You can also get advice about minimising fire losses from your insurer.

THE FIRE SAFETY ORDER

Previous general fire safety legislation

The Regulatory (Fire Safety) Order 2005 replaces previous fire safety legislation.

Any fire certificates issued under the Fire Precautions Act 1971 will cease to have any effect. If a fire certificate has been issued in respect of your animal premises, or the premises were built to recent building regulations, as long as you have made no material alterations and all physical fire precautions have been properly maintained, then it is unlikely you will need to make any significant improvements to your existing physical fire protection arrangements to comply with the Fire Safety Order. However, you must still carry out a fire risk assessment and keep it up to date to ensure that all the fire precautions at your animal premises remain current and adequate.

Note: If you have carried out a fire risk assessment under the Fire Precautions (Workplace) Regulations 1997, and this assessment has been regularly reviewed, then all you will need to do now is revise that assessment, taking into account the wider scope of the Order as described in this guide.

Your premises may also be subject to the provisions of a licence or registration (e.g. under the Riding Establishments Act 1964, amended 1970), and the fire authority may wish to review your risk assessment as part of the licensing approval process.

Fire safety conditions within your premises licence should not be set by a licensing authority where the Order applies.

The Fire Safety Order

The Fire Safety Order applies to England and Wales. Northern Ireland and Scotland have their own laws and Order. It covers general fire precautions and other fire safety duties, which are needed to protect 'relevant persons' in case of fire in and around most 'premises'. The Order requires fire precautions to be put in place 'where necessary' and to the extent that it is reasonable and practicable in the circumstances of the case.

Responsibility for complying with the Fire Safety Order rests with the 'responsible person'. In a workplace, this is the employer and any other person who may have control of any part of the premises, e.g. the occupier or owner. In all other premises the person or people in control of the premises will be responsible. If there is more than one responsible person in any type of premises, all must take all reasonable steps to work with each other.

If you are the responsible person, you **must** carry out a fire risk assessment which must focus on the safety in case of fire of all relevant persons. It should pay particular attention to those at special risk, such as the disabled and those with special needs, and must include consideration of any dangerous substances liable to be on the premises. Your fire risk assessment will need to identify risks that can be removed or reduced and to decide the nature and extent of the general fire precautions you need to take to protect people against the fire risks that remain.

Note: The Fire Safety Order does not include or require the safety of animals from fire to be a mandatory part of your statutory fire risk assessment. However, generally the 'welfare of horses' as discussed in the Government's Horse Strategy Document for England and Wales does include the safety of animals from fire.

If you employ five or more people (regardless of the number of animals present), if your premises are licensed or an alterations notice is in force, you must record the significant findings of the assessment.

There are some other fire safety duties you need to comply with:

- **You must** appoint one or more competent persons, depending on the size and use of your premises, to carry out any of the preventive and protective measures required by the Order. (You can nominate yourself for this purpose.) A competent person is someone with enough training and experience or knowledge and other qualities to be able to implement these measures properly.

- **You must** provide your employees with clear, comprehensive and relevant information on the risks to them identified by the fire risk assessment, about the measures you have taken to prevent fires, and how you will protect them if a fire breaks out.

- **You must** consult your employees (or their elected representatives) about nominating people to carry out particular roles in connection with fire safety and about proposals for improving the fire precautions.

- **You must**, before you employ a child, provide their parent with comprehensive and relevant information on the risks to that child identified by the risk assessment and the measures you have put in place to prevent/protect them from fire and inform any other responsible person of any risks to that child arising from their undertaking.

- **You must** inform non-employees, such as temporary or contract workers, of the relevant risks to them and provide them with information about who are the nominated competent persons and about the fire safety provisions for the premises.

- **You must** co-operate with other responsible persons who also have premises in the building, inform them of any significant risks you find and reduce/control those risks which might affect the safety of their employees.

- **You must** provide the employer of any person from an outside organisation who is working in your premises (e.g. agency providing temporary staff) with comprehensive and relevant information on the risks to those employees and the preventive and protective measures taken. You must also provide those employees with appropriate instructions and relevant information about the risks to them.

- If you are not the employer but have any control of premises which contain more than one workplace, **you are also responsible** for ensuring that the requirements of the Order are complied with in those parts over which you have control.

- **You must** consider the presence of any dangerous substances and the risks this presents to relevant persons from fire.

- **You must** establish a suitable means of contacting the emergency services and provide them with any relevant information about dangerous substances.

- **You must** provide information, instruction and training to your employees, during working hours, about the fire precautions in your workplace when they start working for you and from time to time throughout the period they work for you.

- **You must** ensure that the premises and any equipment provided in connection with firefighting, fire detection and warning or emergency routes and exits are covered by a suitable system of maintenance and are maintained in an efficient state, in efficient working order and in good repair.

- **Your employees must** co-operate with you to ensure the workplace is safe from fire and its effects, and must not do anything that will place themselves or other people at risk.

The above examples outline some of the main requirements of the Order. The rest of this guide will explain how you can meet these requirements.

Responsibilities for short-term hiring or leasing and for shared use

Some animal premises, parts of premises or stables may be leased as an empty and unsupervised facility (e.g. temporary structures and marquees). The fire safety responsibilities of those leasing the premises (and therefore in charge of the activities of those leasing the premises) and those of the owner/leasee need to be established as part of the contract of hire.

In some animal premises and stables (e.g. an indoor arena), parts of the premises may be hired out to another organisation for a separate function or activity. The fire safety responsibilities of those leasing that part of the premises, and therefore in charge of the activities conducted there, and those of the owner/leasee need to be established as part of the contract of hire.

The responsible person for each individual unique, occasional or separate event or function will need to be clearly established and documented, and their legal duties made clear to them. In particular, and where necessary, the responsible person will need to take account of their own lack of familiarity with the layout of the premises, the fire safety provisions and the duties of other responsible persons within the premises.

Who enforces the Fire Safety Order?

The local fire and rescue authority (the fire and rescue service) will enforce the Fire Safety Order in most premises.

The exceptions are:

- Crown-occupied/owned premises where Crown fire inspectors will enforce;

- premises within armed forces establishments where the defence fire service will enforce; and

- certain specialist premises including construction sites, ships (under repair or construction) and nuclear installations, where the Health and Safety Executive (HSE) or local authority will enforce.

The enforcing authority will have the power to inspect your premises to check that you are complying with your duties under the Fire Safety Order. They will look for evidence that you have carried out a suitable fire risk assessment and have acted upon the significant findings of that assessment. If you are required to record the outcome of the assessment, they will expect to see a copy.

If the enforcing authority is dissatisfied with the outcome of your fire risk assessment or the action you have taken, they may issue an enforcement notice that requires you to make certain improvements or, in extreme cases, a prohibition notice that restricts the use of all or part of your premises until improvements are made.

If your premises are considered by the enforcing authority to be or have potential to be high risk, they may issue an alterations notice that requires you to inform them before you make any material alterations to your premises.

Failure to comply with any duty imposed by the Order or any notice issued by the enforcing authority is an offence. You have the right to appeal to a magistrate's court against any notice issued. Where you agree that there is a need for improvements to your fire precautions but disagree with the enforcing authority on the technical solution to be used (e.g. what type of fire alarm system is needed), you may agree to refer this for independent determination.

If having read this guide you are in any doubt about how fire safety laws applies to you, contact the fire safety officer at your local fire and rescue service.

New buildings or significant building alterations should be designed to satisfy current building regulations which address fire precautions. However, you will still need to carry out a fire risk assessment, or review your existing one (and act on your findings), to comply with the Order.

Part 1 Fire risk assessment

MANAGING FIRE SAFETY

Good management of fire safety is essential to ensure that fires are unlikely to occur; that if they do occur they are likely to be controlled quickly, effectively and safely; or that if a fire does occur and grow, everyone in the premises (where possible including animals) is able to escape, including the release of animals inside the premises, to a place of total safety easily and quickly.

Planning

It is of fundamental importance to appreciate that planning for effective fire safety for animal establishments, including for the wide range of indoor and outdoor events, should start at the same time as the planning for all other aspects of day-to-day activities and proposed events.

The planning issues for activities and events can be considered in a number of stages:

- venue design, selection of workers, selection of contractors and subcontractors, construction of marquees, temporary premises, enclosed arenas and seating areas;

- safe delivery and installation of equipment and services which will be used at the premises and/or the event;

- effective fire safety for the duration of the activities;

- safe removal of equipment and services; and

- control of fire risks once the activities are over and the infrastructure is being dismantled or removed.

Good management of fire safety at a temporary or permanent event or activity at an animal establishment will help to ensure that any fire safety matters that arise will always be addressed effectively. Therefore identification of the responsible person is imperative.

The risk assessment that you must carry out will help you ensure that your fire safety procedures, fire prevention measures and fire precautions (plans, systems and equipment) are all in place and working properly, and the risk assessment should identify any issues that need attention. Further information on managing fire safety is available in Part 2.

What is a fire risk assessment?

A fire risk assessment is an organised and methodical look at your animal premises or stables and livery yards, the activities carried on there and the likelihood that a fire could start and cause harm to those in and around the premises.

The terms 'hazard' and 'risk' are used throughout this guide and it is important that you have a clear understanding of how these should be used.

• **Hazard:** Anything that has the potential to cause harm.

• **Risk:** The chance (high, normal or low) of harm occurring.

The aims of the fire risk assessment are:

• to identify the hazards in stables and livery yards;

• to reduce the risk of those hazards causing harm to as low as reasonably practicable; and

• to decide what physical fire precautions and management policies are necessary to ensure the safety of people (and animals) in your buildings if a fire does start.

If your organisation employs five or more people, or your premises are licensed[1] or an alterations notice[2] requiring it is in force, then the significant findings of the fire risk assessment, the actions to be taken as a result of the assessment and details of anyone especially at risk must be recorded. You will probably find it helpful to keep a record of the significant findings of your fire risk assessment even if you are not required to do so.

HOW DO YOU CARRY OUT A FIRE RISK ASSESSMENT?

A fire risk assessment will help you determine the chances of a fire occurring and the dangers from fire that your premises pose for the people (and animals) who use them and for any person in the immediate vicinity. The assessment method suggested shares the same approach as that used in general health and safety legislation and can be carried out either as part of a more general risk assessment or as a separate exercise. As you move through the steps there are checklists to help you.

Before you start your fire risk assessment, stop for a moment, prepare and read through the rest of Part 1 of this guide.

Much of the information for your fire risk assessment will come from the knowledge your employees, colleagues, volunteers and representatives have of the premises, together with experience gained from working in animal premises, stables and at equine events, as well as information given to you by people who have responsibility for other parts of the premises. A tour of all your stable premises will probably be needed to confirm, amend or add detail to your initial views.

It is important that you carry out your fire risk assessment in a practical and systematic way and that you allocate sufficient time to do a proper job. It must take the whole of your animal premises into account, including outdoor locations and any rooms and areas that are rarely used.

---

[1] Appendix E – The glossary offers more information on licences.
[2] See paragraph, page 43 for an explanation of an alterations notice.

If your premises are small, you may be able to assess them as a whole. In larger premises you may find it helpful to divide them into buildings, rooms or a series of assessment areas, using natural boundaries, e.g. the stables, tack rooms, vets' rooms, cooking facilities in staff areas, offices, retail shops, stores, storage barns and residential accommodation (residential accommodation is covered in a separate guidance document). Include the corridors, stairways and all external routes.

If your stables and associated buildings are in a multi-use complex, then the information on hazard and risk reduction will still be applicable to you. However, any alterations to the structure of your individual unit(s) will need to take account of the overall fire safety arrangements in the other sections of the complex.

Your particular animal or equine business may be small in size and limited in the numbers of people or animals present or the level of business activity, but if your operation forms part of a large building with different occupancies then the measures provided by other occupiers may have a direct effect on the adequacy of the fire safety measures in your premises.

Your fire risk assessment should demonstrate that, as far as is reasonable, consideration has been given to the needs of disabled people or people with any impairment.*

*See Part 2, Section 1.14.

FIRE SAFETY RISK ASSESSMENT

1 Identify fire hazards

Identify:
Sources of ignition
Sources of fuel
Sources of oxygen

2 Identify people at risk

Identify:
People in and around the premises
People especially at risk

3 Evaluate, remove, reduce and protect from risk

Evaluate the risk of a fire occurring
Evaluate the risk to people from fire
Remove or reduce fire hazards
Remove or reduce the risks to people
- Detection and warning
- Fire-fighting
- Escape routes
- Lighting
- Signs and notices
- Maintenance

4 Record, plan, inform, instruct and train

Record significant findings and action taken
Prepare an emergency plan
Inform and instruct relevant people; co-operate and co-ordinate with others
Provide training

5 Review

Keep assessment under review
Revise where necessary

Remember to keep to your fire risk assessment under review.

Figure 1: The five steps of a fire risk assessment

STEP 1   IDENTIFY FIRE HAZARDS

The following paragraphs advise you how to identify potential ignition sources and the materials that might fuel a fire.

For a fire to start, three things are needed:

• a source of ignition;

• fuel; and

• oxygen.

1.1   Identify sources of ignition

You can identify the potential ignition sources in your stables and livery yards by looking for possible sources of heat that could get hot enough to ignite materials found at your premises. These sources could include:

• smokers' material, e.g. cigarettes, matches and lighters;

• naked flames, e.g. candles, gas or liquid-fuelled open-flame equipment, such as equipment used by the farrier (mobile or permanent facility) for hot shoeing operations, and hand-held lighting appliances;

• electrical, gas or oil-fired heaters (fixed or portable);

• hot processes, such as decorating or welding by contractors;

• equipment for cooking and preparing refreshments;

• faulty or misused electrical appliances or equipment;

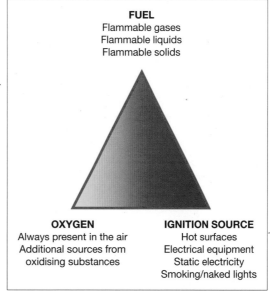

Figure 2: The fire triangle

• lighting equipment, e.g. hand-held liquefied petroleum gas (LPG) and paraffin hand lamps, halogen lamps, display lighting and temporary lighting;

• hot surfaces and the obstruction of fixed ventilation equipment, e.g. the tack room, blanket room or drying room;

• lightning strikes;

• arson; and

• the burning of manure heaps or accumulated combustible rubbish.

Indications of 'near-misses', such as scorch marks on furniture or fittings, discoloured or charred electrical plugs and sockets, cigarette burns, etc, can help you identify hazards which you may not otherwise notice.

1.2 Identify sources of fuel

Anything that burns is fuel for a fire. You need to look for the things that will burn reasonably easily and are in sufficient quantity to provide fuel for a fire or cause it to spread to another fuel source. Some of the most common 'fuels' found in equine establishments are:

- fodder and bedding, e.g. hay, straw, wood shavings, chopped paper and cardboard;

- flammable liquid-based property maintenance and equine presentation materials, such as spirits, paints, varnishes, thinners, adhesives and vegetable-based oils;

- flammable liquids and solvents such as white spirit, methylated spirits, cooking oils and disposable cigarette lighters;

- flammable chemicals such as certain cleaning and dressage products, chemicals and dry cleaning products that use hydrocarbon-based solvents;

- packaging materials, stationery, advertising material, decorations, polystyrene, etc;

- plastics and rubber, such as video tapes, polyurethane foam-filled furniture and polystyrene-based display materials;

- textiles and soft furnishings, such as hanging curtains and clothing displays;

- waste products, particularly finely divided items such as shredded paper and wood shavings, off-cuts and dust;

- flammable gases such as LPG;

- fuel for vehicles;

- central heating fuel; and

- hydraulic oils for agricultural equipment.

You should also consider the materials used to line walls and ceilings, e.g. polystyrene or carpet tiles, fixtures and fittings and how they might contribute to the spread of fire.

Identify sources of oxygen

The main source of oxygen for a fire is in the air around us. In an enclosed building this is provided by the ventilation system in use. This generally falls into one of two categories: natural air flow through doors, windows and other openings in the building; or mechanical air conditioning systems and air handling systems. In many equine buildings there may be a combination of systems, which will be capable of introducing/extracting air to and from the building. A high number of larger equine premises are likely to be affected by high winds that may increase the fire growth rate and fire spread.

Other sources of oxygen at stables and equine establishments may include oxygen cylinders brought in by contractors or the in-house maintenance staff to carry out 'hot work' activities to iron fences, railings, etc.

Checklist

- Have you identified all potential ignition sources?   ☐
- Have you identified all potential fuel sources?   ☐
- Have you identified any additional oxygen supplies/oxidising agents?   ☐
- Have you made a note of your findings?   ☐

STEP 2   IDENTIFY PEOPLE AT RISK

As part of your fire risk assessment, you need to identify those people (and animals) at risk if there is a fire. To do this you need to identify where you have people working at your premises, in permanent working areas or at occasional locations in and around the buildings and yards. You should also consider who else may be at risk, e.g. people on work experience, potential customers, visitors receiving instruction in riding, the public, visiting livery owners, the farrier, contractors, enforcement authority officers, etc, and where these people are likely to be found in and around your stables and yards.

You should pay particular attention to those people who may be especially at risk, such as:

- employees who may work alone, e.g. volunteers, cleaners, security staff, the farrier and vet;

- people who are in isolated areas, e.g. maintenance staff;

- people who are unfamiliar with the premises, e.g. the public, visitors, new livery owners and customers; and

- people with sensory impairments or disabilities, people with other impairments[3] due to alcohol, drugs or medication, and those who may have some other reason for not being able to leave the premises quickly without assistance, e.g. elderly people or parents with children.

In evaluating the risk to people with disabilities or special needs, you may need to discuss individual needs with them. Further guidance on people with special needs is given in Part 2, Section 1.14.

For larger equine buildings used extensively by the public, e.g. indoor arenas, you may need to seek professional advice.

As part of animal welfare, you should also identify all those animals that may be directly or indirectly at risk from fire.

Note: If your premises' fire procedures include the release or rescue of animals still within their stalls or stables by members of your staff and subsequently by the fire service, you should consider what risks these people will face.

[3] Further information can be found at www.drc-gb.org and Supplementary Fire Guide – Means of Escape for disabled people, available at www.communities.gov.uk/fire

STEP 3 EVALUATE, REMOVE, REDUCE AND PROTECT FROM RISK

The management of all the buildings and the way people use them will have an effect on your evaluation of the risks. Management may be your responsibility alone or there may be others, such as the stable owners, proprietors or managing agents, who also have responsibilities.

In multi-occupied premises, all those with some control must co-operate and you need to consider the risks generated by others in the immediate vicinity of the stable buildings.

3.1   Evaluate the risk of a fire occuring

The chances of a fire occurring will be low if your stables have few ignition sources and all combustible materials are kept well away from them.

In general, fires start in one of three ways:

• accidentally, such as when smoking materials are not properly extinguished or when portable heating appliances or lighting displays are knocked over;

• by act or omission, such as when mains electrical equipment is not properly used or maintained, waste packaging is allowed to accumulate near a heat source, cooking and heating operations are misused or neglected, or manure heaps or rubbish are burnt too near to buildings; and

• deliberately, such as an arson attack involving setting fire to the contents of open-sided storage buildings, barns, or external rubbish/refuse bins placed too close to buildings or combustible storage.

Look critically at your premises and try to identify any accidents waiting to happen and any acts or omissions that are likely to allow a fire to start. You should also look for any situation that may present an opportunity for an arsonist by carrying out an arson risk assessment.

Further guidance on evaluating the risk of a fire starting can be found in Part 2, Section 1.

3.2   Evaluate the risk to people and animals from a fire

In Step 2 you identified the people (and animals) likely to be at risk should a fire start anywhere in the premises/stable buildings, and earlier in Step 3 you identified the chances of a fire occurring.

It is unlikely that you will have concluded that there is no chance of a fire starting anywhere in your animal establishment or stables. You now need to evaluate the actual risk to those people (and animals) should a fire start and spread.

When fires start in enclosed spaces such as stables or small storage buildings, the smoke rising from the fire gets trapped by the ceiling or low underside of the roof, and then spreads in all lateral directions to form an ever-deepening layer over the entire room space. The smoke will also pass through any designed and built-in ventilation openings in the roof and end walls, including small holes or gaps in the walls, ceilings and floors, allowing smoke to travel into other parts of the building.

When considering possible incidents, you should also consider the likelihood of any particular incident occurring, but be aware that some very unlikely incidents can put many people (and animals) at risk.

To evaluate the risk to people (and animals) at your premises, you will need to understand the way fire can spread. Fire is spread by three main methods:

• convection;

• conduction; and

• radiation.

There is also a fourth method, which is direct burning. This is where there is either a trailer of fuel travelling from the ignition source to the main fire loading, or, for example, a small fire starts in one corner of the hay barn and, if left unchecked, spreads to the rest of the hay barn and its contents.

Figure 3: Smoke moving through a building

The heat from the fire, unless dissipated, gets trapped in the building and the temperature steadily rises.

Stables that are provided with natural ventilation vents in the roof or side walls will enable limited amounts of smoke from a smouldering fire to dissipate to open air, reducing the potential for smoke logging of the entire floor area.

Smoke produced by a fire also contains toxic gases which are harmful to people (and animals). It is essential that the means of escape and other fire precautions are adequate to ensure that everyone can make their escape to a place of safety, including initial attempts to release the animals from their stalls, before the fire and its effects can trap them in the building.

In evaluating this risk to people (and animals), you will need to consider situations such as:

• fire starting on a lower floor and affecting the only escape route for people on upper floors;

• fire developing in an unoccupied space that people have to pass by to escape from the building;

- fire or smoke spreading through a building via routes such as poorly installed, poorly maintained or damaged vertical shafts, service ducts, ventilation systems, walls, partitions and ceilings;

- fire and smoke spreading through a building due to poor installation of fire precautions, e.g. incorrectly installed fire doors[4] or incorrectly installed services penetrating firewalls and partitions; and

- fire and smoke spreading through the building due to poorly maintained and damaged fire doors, or fire doors allowed to be held or wedged in the open position.

Smoke spreading from a fire will also affect the potential for people to enter the animal premises or stables to rescue and release the animals.

3.3 Remove or reduce the hazards that may cause a fire

Having identified the fire hazards in Step 1, you now need to remove those hazards if reasonably practicable to do so. If you cannot remove the hazards, you need to take reasonable steps to reduce them if you can. This is an essential part of fire risk assessment and, as far as is reasonable, this must take place before any other actions.

Consider any actions you take to remove or reduce fire hazards or risk in light of the effect these actions might have in other areas. For example, if you replace a flammable substance with one that is non-flammable, you must consider whether this might cause harm to people in other ways.

Another example of reducing the risk is not to keep or store any fodder or bedding (hay and straw) inside the animal premises or stables – not even the daily use amount.

Remove or reduce sources of ignition

There are various ways in which you can reduce the risk caused by potential sources of ignition. These include the following:

- Replace naked flame and radiant heaters with fixed convector heaters or a central black heat heating system. Restrict the movement and use of portable heating appliances and guard them.

- Restrict/control the use of naked flames, e.g. camp fires, barbecues, use of candles or other live flame appliances.

[4] Appendix C contains further information on fire doors.

- Resist the practice of burning rubbish and manure heaps.

- Operate a safe smoking policy in designated smoking areas only and prohibit smoking elsewhere.

- Ensure that electrical and mechanical equipment is installed, used, maintained and protected in accordance with the manufacturer's instructions.

- All electrical installations, lighting units, etc should be protected from the effects of dust and cobwebs getting inside the fittings.

- All electrical wiring and equipment should be installed out of reach of animals to prevent them biting and chewing them.

- Control areas where vehicles are parked.

- Take precautions to avoid arson.

Remove or reduce sources of fuel

There are various ways in which you can reduce the risks caused by materials and substances that burn. These include the following:

- Reduce stocks of flammable materials, liquids and gases on display or in storage areas inside the stable buildings, storerooms, etc to the minimum amount required for daily use in the stables. Flammable materials not used during the day should be removed from the building to a suitable storage facility.

- Ensure satisfactory storage and adequate separation distances between flammable materials.

- Remove, cover or treat large areas of highly combustible wall and ceiling linings, e.g. polystyrene or carpet tiles, to reduce the rate of flame spread across the surface.

- Develop a formal system for the control of combustible waste by ensuring that waste materials and rubbish are not allowed to build up and are carefully stored until properly disposed of, particularly at the end of the day.

- Take action to avoid storage areas being located against the outside of buildings as these practices are vulnerable to arson or vandalism.

- Develop a routine cleaning system for the removal of dust and cobwebs from ledges and electrical fittings, including your electrical fire alarm system.

Further guidance on removing and reducing hazards in stables can be found in Part 2, Section 1.

3.4   Remove or reduce the risks to people and animals from a fire

Whatever the assessed level of risk to people from fire, you must, as far as is reasonable, take steps to remove or reduce it.

Further guidance on reducing the risk to people can be found in Part 2, Section 1.

Assessing your residual level of risk

Having removed or reduced your risk of fire to a level as low as reasonably practicable, you should now consider the residual risk from fire and what other measures you need to take.

The level of risk at your animal premises or stables will be a combination of many factors, which include how you manage your premises, the buildings' construction, the activities carried out and the types of people who use your buildings and yards.

In general, animal premises and stables can be categorised as low, normal or high risk simply by determining whether the fire precautions are appropriate to the use and occupancy of the buildings. If your buildings have good fire safety management systems and have been built or refurbished throughout to conform to recent building regulations for their specified use, then the risk rating in the buildings will probably be normal to low.

The following chart will help you decide the residual level of risk in your premises. The red arrow indicates the risk moving higher, and the green arrow indicates lower risk. Having formed a view of the level of risk, you should then consider the measures in the following sections to adequately protect people from the risk of fire.

Higher risk

- Uncoordinated management of animal premises, especially where there is more than one occupier or multiple floor levels, e.g. where fire doors to shared escape routes are regularly wedged open, combustible materials are left in escape routes, fire safety equipment is not maintained, there is a lack of fire safety training and fire procedure drills are not carried out.

- There is the potential for a fire to develop unnoticed and affect escape routes, or the physical constraints of escape routes or low numbers of staff to assist mean that people who are not familiar with the buildings, people with disabilities, parents with young children, elderly people or unaccompanied children would have difficulty leaving the stable buildings.

- Activities involving live flame or highly flammable materials are carried out, or high temperatures are part of the operation, e.g. the farrier's hot shoeing or in staff and public kitchens.

- Large numbers of people may congregate and the premises have not been specifically designed for such numbers. For example, a large barn originally designed for storage only is now being used as an indoor arena with the spectators' seating area discharging into the animal performance areas.

- There is a single unprotected escape route or alternatives are not obvious and may be complex and poorly defined, or may pass through other stable activities or shared areas.

- The premises, particularly in multi-storey buildings, is not divided into separate compartments and fire and smoke could easily spread through open stairways or through other openings, such as holes in the floor or cable/service ducts.

- The physical structure, internal fixtures, fittings, stock and wall and ceiling linings offer a particularly high fire loading or potential for a fire to spread rapidly, e.g. upholstered furniture or storage of bagged animal feed.

- Smoking is allowed in some if not all parts of the building – especially in staff or public areas.

- Open-floor stable premises have low ceilings that may cause rapid fire and smoke spread.

- Heating of the premises is by, or supplemented with, portable or other non-fixed heating appliances such as bar heaters, LPG radiant heaters or mains electric fan heaters.

Normal risk

- The management of the entire animal premises is good and, if the stables are in multiple-occupancy premises, there is co-operation with responsible persons from the other premises. Consideration of fire safety matters, including maintenance and recording, is reliable and regular fire drills and training are carried out.

- The layout of the premises is not complex and escape routes and fire exit routes are clearly marked.

- Escape routes, and in particular stairways, gangways and corridors, are kept clear of combustible materials and obstructions.

- Internal fire doors are normally kept shut and there are no obvious routes through which fire and smoke could easily spread.

- The stables do not contain excessive combustible materials or ignition sources and storage is well organised.

- A suitable automatic fire detection and warning system is installed.

- The animal premises are small, the whole floor area and the access/exit door are visible from every point, and the number of occupants is very low, e.g. a small retail shop, no larger than a corner or very small single-storey high street shop.

Lower risk

- A well managed and maintained single or multi-storey building protected throughout by an automatic sprinkler installation and automatic fire detection and warning system with good fire safety management.

- The physical structure, internal fixtures, fittings, stock and wall and ceiling linings offer limited combustibility and would not add significantly to rapid fire development e.g. purpose built modern office block.

- Smoking is not permitted or is properly controlled in a purpose designed area.

- Housekeeping is good with rubbish and waste stored in a safe and secure locations pending regular disposal.

- The number of people present is low, they are all able-bodied, familiar with the building and the escape routes are visible and short.

- Entry to the stable premises is strictly controlled, visitors and contractors are well informed and managed, with a 'Hot work' and permit to work systems in place.

- The animal premises contain very limited flammable materials or the operation is inherently low risk, e.g. small, single storey, open-plan stables.

3.4.1   Provisions for fire detection and warning systems

It will always be necessary to have some way of detecting a fire and giving warning to all those present at your premises, so that they can escape to a place of ultimate safety before the fire is likely to make the escape routes and the releasing arrangements of the animals unusable/untenable.

In small, open-plan, single-storey animal premises and buildings, a fire may be obvious to everyone as soon as it starts. In these cases, where the number and position of exits and the travel distance to them is adequate, a simple shout of 'fire' or a simple manually operated device, such as a gong, triangle or air horn that can be heard by everybody when operated from any single point within the building or yard, may be all that is needed. Where a simple shout or manually operated device is not adequate, it is likely that an electrical fire warning system is required.

Your fire warning arrangements should take into account warning those people who may be away from the immediate vicinity of the buildings, out in the paddocks or open ménage.

In larger animal premises, particularly those with more than one floor, where an alarm given from any single point is unlikely to be heard throughout all the buildings, an electrical system incorporating sounders and manually operated call points (break-glass boxes should not be used) is likely to be required. This type of system is likely to be acceptable where all parts of the buildings are occupied at the same time and it is unlikely that a fire could start without somebody noticing it quickly. However, where there are unoccupied buildings, areas, common corridors and circulation spaces in multi-occupied buildings in which a fire could develop to the extent that escape routes could be affected before the fire is discovered, automatic fire detection may be necessary.

Figure 4: Sketch of fire alarm frangible cover break

Note: Using audible warning devices may have adverse effects on animals' reactions, thereby making them unpredictable when trying to release them from their stalls. Appropriate visual warning devices may need to be considered and used in lieu of conventional audible sounders in certain locations. Occupiers will also need to consider the arrangements to notify staff in the outside yard areas.

You may also need to consider special arrangements for times when people are working alone, when there are disabled people present or when your normal occupancy patterns are different, e.g. stable staff, the farrier or other contractors working at the weekend or staff attending and checking the horses at night.

In large or complex animal premises, particularly those accommodating large numbers of people and animals or with residential accommodation, it is likely that a more sophisticated form of warning and evacuation, possibly phased, will have to be provided.

If you are not sure that your current arrangements are adequate, you should refer to the additional guidance on fire warning systems in Part 2, Section 2.

Checklist

- Can the existing means of detection ensure a fire is discovered quickly enough to raise an alarm in time for all the occupants to be notified and escape to a safe place? (Delay in discovering a fire may prejudice the potential for the release or rescue of all the animals from their stables or stalls.) ☐

- Can the existing means of warning be clearly heard and/or seen and understood by everyone throughout the stable buildings and yard when initiated from a single point? ☐

- If the fire detection and warning system is electrically powered, does it have a back-up power supply? ☐

- In larger equine establishments that are provided with a public address system, is this system regularly checked at the beginning of each day or activity? ☐

3.4.2   Firefighting equipment

Firefighting equipment can help to protect people (and animals) and reduce the risk of a small fire, e.g. a fire in a wastepaper bin or small pile of bedding or fodder, developing into a large one. This equipment will usually comprise a sufficient number of portable extinguishers, which must be suitable for the risk.

The **safe use** of an appropriate fire extinguisher to control a fire in its early stages can significantly reduce the risk to other people (and animals) in the animal premises. Fire extinguishers are therefore likely to form an essential element in the measures to reduce the risk to people (and animals) from fire.

People with no training in the use of the fire equipment should not attempt to extinguish a fire. You should therefore have a suitable training scheme in place that will enable staff in your premises to safely use the firefighting equipment provided. If your fire strategy means that certain people, e.g. fire marshals/wardens, will be expected to take a more active role, then they should be provided with more comprehensive training.

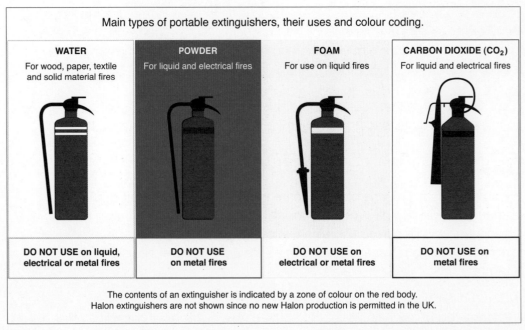

WATER	POWDER	FOAM	CARBON DIOXIDE (CO₂)
For wood, paper, textile and solid material fires	For liquid and electrical fires	For use on liquid fires	For liquid and electrical fires
DO NOT USE on liquid, electrical or metal fires	DO NOT USE on metal fires	DO NOT USE on electrical or metal fires	DO NOT USE on metal fires

The contents of an extinguisher is indicated by a zone of colour on the red body.
Halon extinguishers are not shown since no new Halon production is permitted in the UK.

Figure 5: Types of fire extinguishers

In small animal premises, having one or two portable extinguishers of the appropriate type in an obvious location may be all that is necessary. In larger, more complex animal premises, a greater number of portable extinguishers, sited in obvious locations, such as on the escape routes at each floor level, are likely to be the minimum necessary. It may also be necessary to indicate the location of extinguishers by suitable signs.

Where the firefighting equipment is positioned outside the animal premises, it must be protected from the elements, including extremes of temperature.

Where the firefighting equipment is positioned inside buildings that are vulnerable to dust, it must be suitably covered or protected from settling dust.

Dry powder extinguishers are not suitable for fires involving normal stable bedding materials, particularly if they are used close to animals. Using a dry powder extinguisher near an animal, either inside or outside a building, has the potential to cause respiratory problems for the animal.

Domestic wash-down hoses at very small animal buildings may be acceptable as a suitable firefighting provision providing that:

• the hoses are permanently connected to a reliable water supply of sufficient pressure and fitted with a nozzle that will provide a jet of water not less than 4–5m in length;

• it can reach all the building; and

• where a domestic hose cannot reach all the building, i.e. in excess of 20m, additional suitable hoses from other suitable water supply points are provided, or 9-litre water or AFFF extinguishers are provided.

In small and compact animal premises that are positioned in close proximity to each other, open-top water tanks containing not less than 400 litres of water, provided with buckets of not less than 6 litres capacity, should be provided and kept solely for firefighting.

Some animal premises and stables may have permanently installed firefighting equipment or systems such as fire hose reels, sprinklers or water fog/mist systems.

Other fixed installations and facilities to assist firefighters, such as emergency water supplies and access for fire engines, may also need to be provided.

Further guidance on portable fire extinguishers and other facilities can be found in Part 2, Section 3.1 and on fixed installations in Section 3.2.

Checklist

- Are the extinguishers suitable for the risk and purpose, and are they of sufficient capacity? ☐

- Are there sufficient extinguishers sited throughout all the buildings? ☐

- Are the right types of extinguishers located close to the special fire hazards and can users gain access to them without exposing themselves to risk? ☐

- Are the locations of the extinguishers obvious or does their location or position need indicating? ☐

3.4.3 Escape routes

Once a fire has started, been detected and a warning of fire given, everyone at your premises should be able to escape to a place of safety unaided and without the assistance of the fire and rescue service. (However, some people with disabilities or special needs may need help from other people at the stables.)

The principle upon which escape routes should be designed is to ensure, as far as possible, that any person confronted by fire anywhere in the building should be able to turn away from the fire and escape to a place of relative safety, e.g. direct to open air or to a protected staircase. From there, they will be able to proceed directly to a place of ultimate safety (the assembly point) away from the affected building(s).

In large buildings, marquees and other premises where the animals are contained within individual stalls accessed only via a central aisle down the centre of the building, the occupier will need to consider the safety arrangements for releasing the animals from directly or indirectly affected stalls. This may require a greater number of exit doors than would normally be recommended just for the escape of people from the animal premises, thereby reducing the actual travel distance between the access doors into the building and the stalls. Introducing this practice into the premises' fire procedures will require advice from animal fire safety specialists.

The level of fire protection that should be given to escape routes will vary, depending on the level of risk of fire within the premises and other related factors. Generally, stables that are small, consisting of a single storey, will require fairly simple measures to protect the escape routes compared with larger, multi-storey buildings, which will require a more complex and interrelated system of fire precautions.

It is important at the planning stage for you to consult the local fire and rescue service.

When determining whether your premises have adequate escape routes, you need to consider a number of factors (summarised below), each of which depends on a number of other issues that need to be considered.

The type and number of people using the equine premises, stables and livery yards

The people present at your animal premises or stables will primarily be employees, the vet and the farrier, while at other times there may be a mixture of employees, volunteers, livery owners and members of the public present. Employees can reasonably be expected to have an understanding of the layout of the premises, while other people, particularly in larger yards and premises, will have no or little knowledge of existing or alternative escape routes.

You may want to consider other behavioural issues such as parents seeking their children and people reluctant to abandon their property.

The number and the physical capability of the people present will influence your assessment of the adequacy of the escape routes. You must ensure that your existing escape routes are sufficient to enable the maximum number of people likely to use your buildings at any time, such as during weekends, to escape safely. If necessary, you may need to either increase the capacity of the escape routes or restrict the number of people in the buildings at any one time.

If your stables have low ceilings or low roof undersides, you will need to look critically at how quickly the smoke layers will affect people's judgement and their attempts to reach the nearest exit doors.

It is also important to recognise that animals being released (controlled or not) and people escaping from the premises do not mix. It is therefore important that the escape routes for people are not the same as for the animals.

The designated assembly point(s) should not place people at undue risk from other sources, e.g. arriving fire engines, traffic on a service road, or the need to be in close proximity to released animals or to cross the paths of animals being led to their respective secure areas.

Escape time

Escape routes in any building should be designed so that people can escape quickly enough to ensure they are not placed in any danger from fire. The maximum time normally allowed to escape to a place of relative safety from any premises after a fire warning has been given is about two and a half minutes. Animal premises constructed from timber throughout (treated or otherwise) and with low ceilings should be able to be evacuated in not more than 2 minutes.

Escape times in indoor situations, e.g. marquees and other enclosed structures, are more critical and are controlled by restricting the travel distances to exits. For simplicity, all exit doors, marquee doorway opening flaps, gates, etc should open in the direction of travel and be easily and quickly openable without the need for a key.

The travel distances in Table 2 in Part 2 are based on these escape times.

Age and construction of the premises

The materials from which your animal buildings are constructed and the quality of building work could contribute to the speed with which any fire and smoke may spread, and potentially affect the escape routes the occupants will need to use. A fire starting in a animal building constructed mainly from combustible material will spread faster than one where fire-resisting construction materials have been used.

Depending on the findings of your fire risk assessment, it may be necessary to protect the escape routes against fire and smoke by upgrading the construction of the floors and walls to a fire-resisting standard. You may need to seek advice from a suitably competent person.[5]

Number of escape routes and exits

In general there should normally be at least two escape routes from all parts of the inside of larger animal premises, but in some small stable buildings a single escape route may be acceptable. Where two escape routes are considered necessary, and to further minimise the risk of people becoming trapped, you should ensure that the escape routes are completely independent of each other. This will prevent a fire affecting more than one escape route at the same time.

When evaluating escape routes you may need to build in a safety factor by discounting the largest exit doors from your escape plan, then determine whether the remaining escape routes from a room, floor or building will be sufficient to evacuate all the occupants within a reasonable time. Escape routes from the premises that provide escape in a single direction only may need additional fire precautions to be regarded as adequate.

[5] See Appendix E – Glossary.

Exit doors on escape routes should normally open in the direction of travel and be quickly and easily opened without the need for a key. Checks should be made to ensure that final exits are of sufficient width to accommodate the number of people who may use the escape routes they serve.

Your fire risk assessment should also consider the adequacy of the existing stable doors in respect of staff and firefighters entering the buildings to release the animals from their stalls, and then lead or usher them from the building. Doors in stables should not be less than 2.4 m high and 1.2 m wide.

Management of escape routes

It is essential that all fire escape routes and their safeguards are managed and maintained to ensure that they remain usable and available at all times when the premises are occupied. All animal staff and volunteers should be made aware of the escape routes within the premises through regular staff training sessions.

Figure 6:
Picture of blocked corridor

Gangways, isles between stalls, internal corridors and stairways that form part of escape routes should be kept clear and hazard free at all times. Items that may be a source of fuel or pose an ignition risk should never be located in isles between stalls, corridors, gangways or stairways that will be used as an escape route and/or an animal release route.

For more detailed information on escape routes, please refer to Part 2, Section 4.

Checklist

- Is the construction of your animal premises, particularly in the case of multi-storey buildings, such that, in the event of fire, heat and smoke will not spread uncontrolled through the building to the extent that people are unable to use the escape routes? ☐

- Are any holes or gaps in walls, ceilings and floors properly sealed, e.g. where services such as ventilation ducts and electrical cables pass through them? ☐

- Can all the occupants escape to a place of safety in a reasonable time? ☐

- Are the existing escape routes adequate for the numbers and type of people who may need to use them, e.g. members of the public, disabled people and people leading animals? ☐

- Are the exits in the right place and do the escape routes lead as directly as possible to the outside to a place of safety? ☐

- In the event of a fire, could all available exits be affected or will at least one route from any part of the premises remain available? ☐

- Are the seals around the internal fire doors intact and do self-closing devices work, where fitted, properly? ☐

- Releasing each animal from their individual stalls can be time consuming, especially if they are not wearing any head harnesses to lead them out. Are the existing numbers of exit doors sufficient for all the animals to be released from their stalls and discharged from the building within 5 to 7 minutes? ☐

- Are the number and width of the existing fire exit doors suitable for use by people, including those people with special needs, and are these doors also suitable for use by animals? ☐

- Can all the occupants escape to a place of total safety in a reasonable time? ☐

- Are all the escape routes and the outside of final exits kept clear at all times? ☐

- Do the required and identified emergency doors open in the direction of escape? ☐

- Can all final fire exit doors and gates be opened easily and immediately in the event of an emergency? ☐

- Have you made arrangements to ensure that all the fire precautions within the animal premises are properly maintained and available for use when required? ☐

- Are people who work in the building aware of the importance of maintaining the safety of the escape routes, e.g. by ensuring that any fire doors are not wedged open and that combustible materials are not stored within escape routes? ☐

- If you have fire exit doors with fastenings that are operated from the inside of the animal premises but have also been identified as access doors for staff to enter the building to release the animals, can these doors be quickly and easily opened from the outside in an emergency? ☐

3.4.4   Escape lighting

People at your animal premises must be able to find their way to a place of safety in the event of a fire by using identified escape routes that have sufficient levels of lighting. If some of your escape exit routes are internal and without windows, or your premises are used during periods of darkness, including early darkness on winter days, then some form of safe emergency lighting is likely to be required.

In some very simple or small animal premises located in urban or built-up areas, where back-up to the normal lighting is necessary and where there are simple escape routes and few members of staff or public, borrowed lighting, e.g. from street lamps where they illuminate escape routes, may be acceptable. Where borrowed lighting is not available, particularly in remote or isolated areas, suitably placed torches may be acceptable.

Where a back-up system is required in larger, more complex animal premises, it is likely that a more comprehensive system of automatic emergency lighting will be needed to illuminate all the escape routes.

Where people have difficulty seeing conventional signs, a 'way-finding' system may need to be considered.

Where members of the stables' staff and firefighters will be expected to enter animal accommodation buildings to release and evacuate the animals, the level of emergency lighting may have to be increased to a level that will enable nominated staff and rescuers to see their way into the premises, release the animals and lead them outside.

Emergency lighting should also be provided in the external yard areas and evacuation assembly points.

Further guidance is available in Part 2, Section 5.

Checklist

- Are your premises likely to be visited and used during periods of darkness? ☐

- Do all the internal and external escape routes have sufficient levels of lighting? ☐

- Do the external yard areas have sufficient levels of emergency lighting? ☐

- Is the level of lighting adequate for people to see to safely release and evacuate the animals? ☐

- Have you provided emergency escape lighting by means of either an independent back-up power supply to the normal lighting or by means of separate lighting with an independent source? ☐

3.4.5   Signs and notices

Signs must be used, where necessary, to help people identify escape routes and find firefighting equipment, fire warning arrangements and emergency fire telephones. These signs are required under the Health and Safety (Safety Signs and Signals) Regulations 1996 and must comply with the provisions of those Regulations.

For a sign to comply with these Regulations, it must be in pictogram form. The pictogram can be supplemented by text if this is considered necessary to make the sign easily understood, but you must not have a safety sign that uses only text.

Figure 7: Typical fire exit sign

Notices must be used, where necessary, to provide instructions on how to use any fire safety equipment, the actions to be taken in the event of fire, and to assist the fire and rescue service.

Where the locations of escape routes and firefighting equipment are readily apparent and the firefighting equipment is visible at all times, then signs are not necessary. In all other situations, it is likely that the fire risk assessment will indicate that signs will be necessary.

Locations and storage areas containing chemicals, flammable liquids and gases must be suitably identified by appropriate hazard signage.

All signs and notices should be positioned so that they can be easily seen and understood.

For more information on safety signs and notices, please refer to Part 2, Section 6.

Checklist

- Are all escape routes and exits, the locations of firefighting equipment, fire warning arrangements and emergency fire telephones adequately indicated by appropriate signs? ☐

- Have you provided notices such as those giving information on how to operate security devices on exit doors, those indicating that fire doors must be kept shut and fire action/procedure notices for staff and other people? ☐

- Are you maintaining all the necessary signs and notices so that they continue to be correct, legible and understood? Particular attention should be paid to those signs and notices located in dusty environments. ☐

- Are you maintaining signs that you have provided for the information of the fire and rescue service, such as those indicating the location of emergency water supplies, water suppression system stop valves, the storage of hazardous substances, isolating valves and switch gear to the electricity and gas supplies? ☐

3.4.6   Testing and maintenance

You need to keep any equipment, devices or facilities that are provided at your stables for the safety of people and animals, such as fire warning arrangements, provision for fighting fire, artificial and emergency lighting, fire exits and fire doors, in effective working order. Check that signs are legible and, where practicable, that all emergency lighting units are in place and in working order.

You need to ensure that regular checks, periodic servicing and maintenance are carried out, whatever the size of your premises, and any defects are put right as quickly as possible.

You, or a person you have nominated, can carry out certain checks and routine maintenance work. Further maintenance may need to be carried out by a competent service engineer. Where contractors are used, third party certification is one method whereby a reasonable assurance of quality of work and competence can be achieved.[6]

The following are examples of checks and tests that should be carried out.

Daily checks

Bolts, security devices and other types of door fastening arrangements on fire exit doors[7] and fire escape routes should be checked to ensure that they can be quickly and easily opened by all people in an emergency and are clear from obstructions and combustible materials.

Where exit doors have been fitted with a security padlock installed for the building's security outside working hours, the padlock should be removed during the periods when the building is occupied.

Check the fire alarm panel to ensure the system is active, fully operational and not giving regular false alarms. Where practicable, visually check that emergency lighting units are in good repair and apparently working. Check that all safety signs and notices are clean, conspicuous and legible.

Weekly tests

Comprehensive fire detection and warning systems and manually operated warning devices should be tested weekly following the manufacturer's or installer's instructions.

Check the batteries of safety torches and that fire extinguishers and hose reels are not covered in dust, are correctly located and are in reliable working order.

Where fire pumps and standby generators are installed, they should be tested for at least 3 minutes each week.

Monthly tests

Test all emergency lighting systems and safety torches for sufficient charge and illumination in accordance with the manufacturer's or supplier's instructions.

---

[6] Further information on third party certification can be obtained from UKAS at www.ukas.com
[7] See Appendix C for information on security on exit doors.

Six-monthly tests

The fire detection, fire warning and emergency/escape lighting systems should be tested and maintained by a competent person.

Annual tests

The emergency lighting and all the firefighting equipment, fire warning arrangements and other installed fire safety systems should be tested and maintained by a competent person.

Note: The examples of testing and maintenance given above are not intended to be prescriptive and other testing regimes may be appropriate.

Keeping records of the maintenance arrangements carried out will help you demonstrate to the enforcing authority that you have complied with the statutory requirements of the fire safety legislation.

Further information on maintenance and testing can be found in Part 2.

Appendices A and B give details of sample checklists that you can use.

Other equipment and facilities, including those for firefighters

In some larger animal premises, fixed fire control equipment such as sprinklers, water fog and carbon dioxide extinguishing systems, and facilities such as emergency water supplies and access roads for fire engines, may have been provided for the safety of people and animals in the stable buildings and to assist firefighters. Where these have been required by law, e.g. building regulations or local acts, such systems will need to be maintained.

In most cases it will be necessary to consult a competent service engineer. See Part 2, Section 3 for further information.

Checklist

- Do you regularly check all fire exit doors, escape routes and associated lighting and exit signage? ☐
- Do you regularly check all your firefighting equipment and provisions? ☐
- Do you regularly check your fire detection and alarm warning equipment? ☐
- Do you regularly check any other equipment provided to help maintain the escape routes? ☐
- Have you determined whether your emergency/escape lighting is adequate? ☐
- Are those who test and maintain the fire safety equipment qualified and properly trained to do so? ☐
- Are you maintaining any facilities, water supplies and access roads that have been provided for the safety of people in the building and for the use of firefighters? ☐

STEP 4 RECORD, PLAN, INFORM, INSTRUCT AND TRAIN

In Step 4 there are four further elements of the risk assessment you should focus on in order to address the management of fire safety at your animal premises. In smaller animal premises this could be done as part of the day-to-day management; however, as the premises or operations become larger, it may be necessary for a formal structure and written policy to be developed, further details of which can be found in Part 2, Section 7.1.

4.1   Record significant findings and action taken

If five or more people are employed, your animal premises holds a licence, or an alterations notice requiring you to do so is in force, you must record the significant findings of your fire risk assessment and the actions you have taken. Even in small animal premises where you are not required to record the significant findings, it is considered good practice to do so.

In some very small stables and livery yards, record keeping may be no more than a few sheets of paper (possibly forming part of the stables' health and safety folder), containing details of significant findings and any action taken and a copy of the stables' emergency plan.

At larger animal establishments it is best to keep a dedicated record, including details of significant findings, any action taken, maintenance of fire protection equipment and training, and a copy of the emergency plan. There is no one 'correct' format specified.

It might be helpful to include a simple line drawing to illustrate your precautions. This can also help you check your fire precautions as part of your ongoing review.

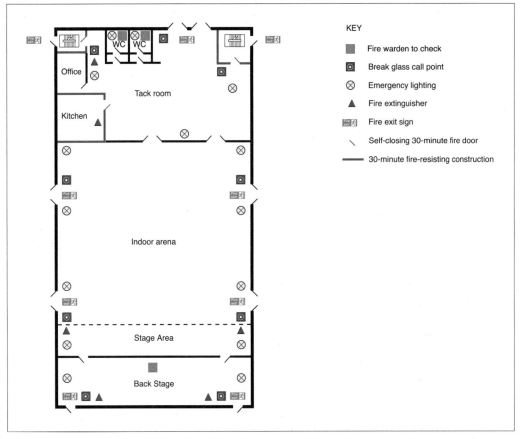

KEY

■ Fire warden to check

⊡ Break glass call point

⊗ Emergency lighting

▲ Fire extinguisher

🏃 Fire exit sign

╲ Self-closing 30-minute fire door

── 30-minute fire-resisting construction

Figure 8: Example of a line drawing showing general fire safety precautions

The record could also take the form of a simple list, which may or may not be supported by a simple plan of the premises.

Step 1	Step 2	Step 3	Step 4
Significant findings of fire hazards	People who are at risk from the hazards (You may wish to include the animals)	Remove or reduce the risk and introduce measures to protect any residual risks	Further action needed Training, information, instruction and co-ordination
Electrical heaters in the stalls too near combustible materials	Visitors, volunteers and staff (You may wish to include the animals)	Ensure a minimum distance of 1m between lamp and combustible material 2kg carbon dioxide fire extinguisher provided in the stables	Staff informed of hazards from the heaters Staff trained to use fire extinguisher

You must be able to satisfy the enforcing authority, if called upon to do so, that a suitable and sufficient fire risk assessment has been undertaken. Keeping records will help you do this and will also form the basis of your subsequent reviews. If you keep records, you do not need to record all the details, only those that are significant and the action you have taken.

The findings of your fire risk assessment will help you develop your emergency plan, the instruction, information and training you need to provide, the co-operation and co-ordination arrangements you may need to have with other responsible people, and the arrangements for maintenance and testing of your fire precautions. If you are required to record the significant findings of your fire risk assessment, then these arrangements must also be recorded. Information on these arrangements is given below in Sections 4.2 to 4.4.

Additional information and examples of recording can be found in Part 2, Section 7.

Checklist

• Have you recorded the significant findings of your assessment? ☐

• Have you recorded what you have done to remove or reduce the risk? ☐

• Are your records readily available for inspection by the enforcing authority? ☐

4.2   Emergency plans

The purpose of an emergency plan is to ensure that the people in your stables and yard know what to do if there is a fire and to ensure that people can be safely evacuated from your stables and animals can be safely released.

If five or more people are employed, your stables are licensed or an alterations notice requiring it is in force, then details of your emergency plan must be recorded. Even if it is not required, it is good practice to keep a record.

Your emergency plan should be based on the outcome of your fire risk assessment and be available for your employees, their representatives (where appointed), volunteers and the enforcing authority.

Where young people are involved, their parents or guardians will need to be informed.

In small animal premises and yards, the emergency plan may be no more than a fire action notice, as shown below.

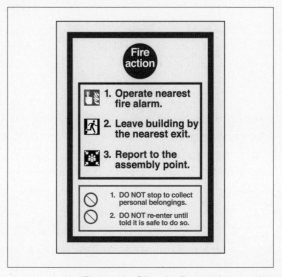

Figure 9: Simple fire action notice

In larger and more complex animal premises, the emergency plan will need to be more detailed and compiled only after consultation with other occupiers and other responsible people, e.g. tenants or livery owners, who have control over parts of the premises. In most cases this means that a single emergency plan covering all the buildings will be necessary.

It will help if you can agree on one person to co-ordinate this task.

Your emergency plan should be appropriate to your stables and could include:

- how people will be warned if there is a fire;

- the action the staff should take if they discover a fire;

- how the evacuation of the premises should be carried out;

- how the release and evacuation of the animals should be carried out:

- identification of the secure areas where the animals should be taken to, away from the fire;

- where staff should assemble after they have left the buildings and procedures for checking whether all the buildings have been evacuated;

- identification of key escape routes, how people can gain access to them and escape from them to a place of safety;

- arrangements and provisions for fighting fire;

- the duties and identities of staff who have specific responsibilities in the event of a fire;

- arrangements for the safe evacuation of people identified as being especially at risk, such as contractors, those with disabilities, members of the public and visitors;

- any machines, processes or power supplies that need to be stopped or isolated in the event of a fire;

- specific arrangements, if necessary, for high fire risk areas;

- contingency plans for when life safety systems, e.g. fire detection and alarm systems, sprinklers or smoke control systems, are out of order;

- how the fire and rescue service and any other emergency services will be called and who will be responsible for doing this;

- procedures for opening gates to the roadway and yard;

- procedures for meeting the fire and rescue service on their arrival and notifying them of any special risks, e.g. the location of highly flammable materials; and

- what training employees need and the arrangements for ensuring that this training is given.

If you have larger or more complex equine premises, it might be helpful for you to include a simple line drawing. This can also help you check your fire precautions as part of your ongoing review.

Checklist

- Do you have an emergency plan and, where necessary, have you recorded the details? ☐

- Does your plan take account of other responsible people in your buildings? ☐

- Is the plan readily available for all staff to read? ☐

- Is the emergency plan available to the enforcing authority? ☐

4.3   Information, instruction, co-operation and co-ordination

You must give comprehensible and relevant information and appropriate instructions to your staff and the employers of other people working at your stables about how to prevent fires and what they should do if a fire does occur. If you intend to employ a child, you must inform the parents of the significant risks you have identified and the precautions you have taken.

You must also co-operate and co-ordinate with other responsible people who use any part of your premises. It is unlikely that your emergency plan will work without this.

Information and instruction

All staff, including volunteers, should be given information and instruction as soon as possible after appointment and regularly thereafter. Make sure you include all staff who work outside normal working hours, such as the farrier, cleaners or maintenance staff.

The information and instruction you give must be in a form that can be used and understood. They should take account of those with learning difficulties or disabilities such as hearing or sight impairment, those with learning difficulties and those who do not normally use English as their first language.

The information and instruction you give should be based on your emergency plan and must include:

- the significant findings from your fire risk assessment;

- the measures that you have put in place to reduce the risk;

- the action all staff and volunteers should take in the event of a fire;

- the identity of people you have nominated with responsibilities for fire safety;

- the identity of people you have nominated with the responsibility of releasing the animals; and

- special considerations for serious and/or imminent dangerous situations.

At small animal premises, where no significant risks have been identified and there are only limited numbers of staff, information and instruction may simply involve an explanation of the fire procedures and how they are to be applied. This should include showing the staff the fire protection arrangements, including the designated escape routes, emergency animal release arrangements, the location and operation of the fire warning system and any other fire safety equipment provided, such as provisions for fighting fire. Fire action notices can complement this information and, where used, should be posted in prominent locations, e.g. staff accommodation, offices, inside the animal premises, etc.

In larger animal premises, it will be necessary for written instructions to be given to people who have been nominated to carry out a designated safety task, such as calling the fire and rescue service or checking that the inside and outside of the exit doors are in proper working order and free from obstruction at the start of each working day.

Further guidance on information and instruction to staff and information on working with animals, chemicals and dangerous substances can be found in Part 2, Section 7.4.

Co-operation and co-ordination

In small, owner-occupied animal premises, you are likely to be solely responsible. However, in stables owned by someone else, or where there is more than one occupier, and others are responsible for different parts of the animal premises, it is important that you liaise with them and inform them of any significant risks that you have identified. By liaising, you can co-ordinate your resources to ensure that your actions and working practices do not place other people or animals at risk in the event of a fire, and that a co-ordinated emergency plan operates effectively.

Where two or more responsible people share the animal premises in which a rapidly developing fire may occur, the responsible person with overall responsibility for the premises must co-ordinate any measures necessary to protect people and animals from any risk that may arise.[8]

All employees and volunteers also have a responsibility to co-operate with their employer so far as it is necessary for the employer to comply with any legal duty.

Further information on co-operation and co-ordination can be found in Part 2, Section 7.4.

---

[8] See details of HSE guidance, successful health and safety management, in Appendix E.

Checklist

- Have you told all your staff and volunteers about the premies' emergency plan, including the identity of people you have nominated to do particular tasks? ☐

- Have you given staff and volunteers information about any dangerous substances? ☐

- Have you given staff and volunteers information about any excitable or unpredictable animals that may have to be released? ☐

- Do you have arrangements for informing livery owners and temporary or agency staff? ☐

- Do you have arrangements for informing other employers whose staff are guest workers at your premises, such as the farrier, maintenance contractors, etc? ☐

- Have you co-ordinated your fire safety arrangements with any other responsible people in your buildings? ☐

- Have you recorded the details of the information or instructions you have given, and the details of any arrangements for co-operation and co-ordination with others you have undertaken? ☐

4.4   Fire safety training

You must provide adequate fire safety training for all your staff. The type of training should be based on the particular features of your stables, including type and location, and should:

- take account of the findings of the fire risk assessment;

- explain your emergency procedures;

- explain the emergency procedures for the release of the animals and where they should be taken;

- take account of work activities and explain the duties and responsibilities of staff;

- take place during working hours and be repeated periodically where appropriate; and

- be easily understandable by your staff and other people who may be present.

In small animal premises this may be no more than showing new staff and volunteers the fire exits and giving basic training on what to do in the event of fire. In larger animal premises, such as large livery, public riding or polo stables with a reasonable staff turnover and staff working out of hours and in shifts, the organisation of fire safety training will need to be planned.

Your fire procedure training should include the following:

- the action to take on discovering a fire;

- how to raise the alarm and what happens then;

- the action to take upon hearing the fire alarm;

- the procedures for alerting members of the public, visitors and contractors, including, where appropriate, directing them to exits;

- the arrangements and who is responsible for calling the fire and rescue service;

- the evacuation procedures for everyone in all your animal buildings to reach the assembly point(s) at a safe location;

- the release and securing of the animals in identified enclosures;

- the location and, when appropriate, use of the provided firefighting equipment (if safe to do so);

- the location of escape routes, especially those not in regular use;

- recognising all the escape doors and how to open them;

- the importance of keeping fire-resisting doors closed to prevent the spread of fire, heat and smoke;

- where appropriate, how to stop machines and processes and isolate power supplies in the event of a fire (if safe to do so);

- the reason for not using lifts, if installed (except those specifically installed or nominated, following a suitable fire risk assessment, for the evacuation of people with disabilities);

- the safe use and risks of storing or working with highly combustible, flammable liquids and gases; and

- the importance of general fire safety practices, which include good housekeeping.

All the employees and volunteers identified in your emergency plan who have a supervisory role in the event of a fire (e.g. fire marshals or wardens and, in larger animal premises and yards, fire parties or teams), should be given details of your fire risk assessment and receive additional training.

Further guidance on training needs, together with examples of how to carry out a fire drill, can be found in Part 2, Section 7.5.

Checklist

- Have your staff and volunteers received any fire safety training? ☐

- When did you last carry out a fire drill? ☐

- Did your fire drill include the release of the animals? ☐

- Are employees aware of specific tasks in the event of a fire? ☐

- Are you maintaining a record or logbook of training sessions? ☐

- Do you carry out joint training and fire drills with the other occupiers of the stables or yard? ☐

- If you use or store hazardous or highly flammable substances, have your staff received appropriate training? ☐

STEP 5　REVIEW

If you have any reason to suspect that your last fire risk assessment is no longer valid or there has been a significant change at your stables that has affected your existing fire precautions, you will need to review your assessment and, if necessary, revise it.

Such changes could include:

- admitting members of the public to indoor arenas, the number of stables or the number of horses kept, or the way in which you organise them, including the introduction of new equipment;

- alterations to the animal premises, including the internal layout, increasing fire loading;

- substantial changes to furniture and fixings;

- the introduction, change of use or increase in the storage of flammable materials or other hazardous substances;

- the failure of any fire precautions, e.g. fire detection/warning systems, life safety or property protection sprinklers or ventilation systems;

- significant changes to quantities of stock, fodder or bedding, etc;

- a significant increase in the number of people likely to be present at any one time;

- the introduction of residential accommodation;

- the presence of people with any form of disability or impairment; and

- incidents at other animal establishments or stables that injured, or could have injured, people or animals and from which lessons could be learnt and preventive action taken.

You should also consider the potential risk of any significant changes before they are introduced. It is usually more effective to minimise a risk by, for example, ensuring adequate, appropriate storage space for items before they are introduced to your premises.

Do not amend your assessment for every trivial change, but if a change introduces new hazards you should consider them and, if significant, do whatever you need to keep the risks under control. In any case, you should keep your assessment under review to make sure that the precautions are still working effectively. You may find it convenient to re-examine the fire prevention and protection measures at the same time as your animal premises' health and safety assessment.

If a fire or 'near miss' occurs, this could indicate that your existing assessment may be inadequate and you should carry out a re-assessment. It is good practice to identify the cause of any incident and then review and, if necessary, revise your fire risk assessment in the light of this.

Records of testing, maintenance and training, etc are useful aids in a review process. See Appendix A for an example.

Alterations notices

If you have been served with an 'alterations notice', check it to see whether you need to notify the enforcing authority about any changes you propose to make as a result of your review. If the changes you propose to make include building work, you should consult the building control body.[9]

END OF PART 1

You should now have completed the five-step fire risk assessment process using the additional information in Part 2 where necessary. In any review you may need to revisit Steps 1 to 4.

[9] Further information on alterations notices is provided in 'An introduction to the Fire Safety Order'.

Part 2 Further guidance on fire risk assessment and fire precautions

Section 1 Further guidance on fire risks and preventative measures

This section provides further information on evaluating the risk of a fire and its prevention at your animal premises. You should spend time developing long-term workable and effective strategies to reduce hazards and the risk of a fire starting. At its simplest, this means separating flammable materials from ignition sources. You should consider the following matters.

1.1 Housekeeping

For many small animal premises, good housekeeping will lower the chances of a fire occurring. Consequently, the accumulation of combustible materials in animal premises should be monitored carefully.

Figure 11: Example of poor housekeeping at open air events

Figure 12: Bins under a stairway (courtesy of Cheshire fire and rescue service)

Refuse

Waste material should be kept in suitable containers prior to removal from the premises. If bins, particularly wheeled bins, are used outside, they should be secured in a compound to prevent them being moved to a position next to the building and set on fire. Skips and waste bins should never be placed against any building and should normally be a minimum of 6m away from any part of the premises.

If you generate considerable quantities of combustible waste material, then you may need to develop a formal plan to manage this effectively.

Large accumulations of manure should be monitored; the practice of placing manure compounds up against buildings should be discouraged.

The practice of burning manure to prevent landfill disposal should be carefully reviewed.

1.2 Storage

Most of the stocks of fodder and bedding or other materials found at stables will be combustible. If your animal premises have inadequate or poorly managed bulk storage areas, then the risk of fire is likely to be increased. Excessive stock adds to the material available to fuel a fire.

Only the day-to-day quantities of fodder and bedding materials should be kept inside the buildings, and even then this practice should be carefully monitored and constantly reviewed.

Combustible materials are not just those materials generally regarded as highly combustible, such as hay and straw, but also all materials that will readily catch fire. However, by carefully considering the type of material, the quantities kept and the storage arrangements employed, the risks can be significantly reduced with careful planning.

Figure 13: An example of poor storage

In the animal premises' offices, the retention of large quantities of paper records, especially if not filed away in proprietary cabinets, can increase the fire hazard. Such readily available flammable material makes the potential effect of arson more serious.

Many premises will take great care to present an efficient and attractive image in all the animal and yard areas, while the bedding and fodder storage areas are usually neglected and are allowed to become over-stocked or dumping areas for unwanted items such as vehicles, gas cylinders, general materials, etc.

Care should be taken to ensure that combustible materials are not piled up or placed against electrical equipment or heaters, even if turned off for the summer.

Smoking should not be allowed in any of the stable buildings or outside areas.

To reduce the risk of fire, you should store excess amounts of combustible materials and stock inside storerooms or cupboards in dedicated storage areas, compounds and barns.

All storage barns and buildings and garages for vehicles should be structurally separate from buildings that accommodate people and animals.

Do not store excess stock in areas where the public or visitors would normally have access.

The manner of displaying stock in any retail shops and any additional risk of fire that this generates should be evaluated. For example, rugs and blankets stacked on the floor on top of each other would not present a high fire risk, but bundles of blankets wrapped in polythene protective covers and stored vertically up against a wall or hung on display racks present a vertical surface for fire to spread rapidly upwards. The display of large quantities of waterproof clothing on vertical hangers is also likely to increase the risk of rapid fire development.

Your fire risk assessment should also consider any additional risks generated by seasonal products such as Christmas decorations.

Action to reduce these risks could include:

* ensuring that such areas are adequately controlled and monitored;

* using inherently fire-resistant display materials wherever possible (suppliers should be able to provide evidence of this); and

* ensuring that electrical lighting fittings used as part of the sales display do not become a potential source of ignition.

1.3 Storage and use of dangerous substances

The storage of flammable materials, liquids and gases is controlled by other legislation in addition to this fire safety law and you should ensure this is complied with at all times.[10]

Dangerous substances are generally those materials, gases, vegetable oils, liquids, dusts and other preparations that are highly flammable, oxidising or potentially explosive.

Where there are large quantities of highly combustible materials, particularly when they are easily ignitable, you should consider the following ways of removing or reducing the risk from fire:

* Reduce combustible materials, i.e. hay and straw kept in the same building or areas as the animals, to the smallest reasonable amount necessary for operating the daily business.

---

[10] Chemicals (Hazard Information and Packaging for Supply) Regulations 2002; The Approved Supply List; The Approved Classification and Labelling Guide 2002; and the Dangerous Substances and Explosive Atmospheres Regulations 2002.

- Substitute highly combustible materials with less combustible ones.

- Store highly combustible materials and flammable liquids in fire-resisting enclosures or containers.

Flammable liquids

Flammable liquids can present a higher risk of fire, particularly if not well managed, because they can flow and spread, either in liquid form or by giving off vapours, and so the opportunity to find an ignition source is greatly increased.

A leak from a container of flammable liquid, such as petrol or methylated spirits on the stable, tack room or store floor, can fill low-level areas with flammable vapours and lead to a fire when electrical or heating equipment is automatically turned on. A small fire adjacent to a cabinet of methylated spirits or white spirit in the tack room could rapidly develop as the plastic containers begin to melt and spill their flammable contents.

Figure 14: A 50-litre flammable storage bin

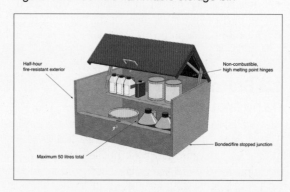

If the use of flammable liquids is essential, then no more than half a day's supply should be kept available at the point of use and this should be kept in sealed containers.

Greater quantities can be stored in a proprietary fire-resisting storage bin that will contain any leaks.

For quantities of flammable liquids above 50 litres (aggregate amount), a properly constructed and designated ventilated storage facility or a secure open-air compound should be used. In such situations you should seek advice from a competent person.

Figure 15: A fire-resisting pedal bin for rags

No more than a total of 70kg of flammable gases, e.g. LPG, should be stored or displayed within the stable premises, and this quantity should be reduced to 15kg if the stables are adjacent to or beneath residential accommodation.

Further guidance on the safe storage of LPG is available from your supplier or the Liquid Petroleum Gas Association.[11]

If your animal premies are likely to have significant quantities of flammable liquid vapours present, you should seek expert advice about safe powered ventilation equipment and safe electrical equipment. Such equipment will probably include suitable fire warning and emergency lighting systems.

All flammable liquids and gases should be locked away, especially when the stables are unoccupied, to reduce the chance of them being used in an arson attack.

Piping

Piping conveying gas or liquid should be, as far as practicable, of rigid material.

Any necessary piping should consist of a material suitable for the gas or liquid being conveyed, and adequately reinforced to resist crushing and withstand the maximum internal pressure to which it may be subjected. Any connections to flexible piping should be of an approved type or pattern (i.e. screwed or otherwise secured to prevent accidental disconnection).

---

[11] Liquefied Petroleum Gas Association, Code of practice 7: Storage of full and empty LPG cylinders and cartridges.

1.4 Equipment and machinery

Lack of preventive maintenance increases the risk of fire starting in machinery. Common causes of fire in mains electrical equipment are:

- allowing ventilation points to become clogged or blocked, causing overheating;

- allowing extraction equipment in catering environments (kitchens) to build up excessive grease deposits;

- loose drive belts or lack of lubrication of machinery leading to increased friction;

- disabling or interfering with mechanical equipment's automatic or manual safety features and cut-outs; and

- leaking valves, glands or joints allowing fuel oil and other flammable liquids to contaminate the ground, floors or goods.

A competent person should adequately and regularly maintain machinery, equipment and plant, including cooking, lighting and heating equipment, and office equipment such as photocopiers. Appropriate signs and instructions on the safe use of the equipment may be necessary.

1.5 Electrical safety

All mains electrical equipment is a potential significant cause of accidental fires in stables, storerooms, shops and offices. The main causes are:

- overheating cables and equipment, e.g. due to overloading;

- incorrect installation or use of equipment;

- lack of maintenance or testing;

- damaged or inadequate insulation on cables or wiring;

- combustible materials being placed too close to electrical equipment, which may give off heat even when operating normally or may become hot due to a fault;

- arcing and sparking of electrical equipment and installations; and

- damage to the building's electrical wiring from horses chewing on the installation.

All electrical equipment provided at stables should be installed and maintained in a safe manner by a competent person. If portable electrical appliances and equipment are used, including items brought into a workplace by the animal premises' staff and volunteers, then your fire risk assessment should ensure that it undergoes portable appliance testing ('PAT') prior to its use and at suitable intervals.[12]

If you have any doubt about the safety of your premises' electrical installation, then you should consult a competent electrician.

1.6 Smoking

Carelessly discarded cigarettes and other smoking materials can be a major cause of fire at animal premises. A cigarette can smoulder for several hours, especially when surrounded by combustible material. Many fires are started several hours after the smoking materials have been emptied into waste bags and left for future disposal.

You should consider prohibiting smoking in and outside all your premises. If smoking is allowed in your premises, designated smoking areas should be provided well away from all buildings, including open-air manèges with combustible floor or ground coverings. People stubbing out their lighted cigarette ends on combustible ground coverings can cause a smouldering fire.

Suitable signs should be displayed throughout all buildings informing people of the animal premises' smoking policy and the locations where smoking is permitted.

Tack cleaning and storerooms often double up as staff rooms, where smoking is normally allowed. This practice should be reviewed.

In those areas where smoking is permitted, the provision of deep and substantial ashtrays will help prevent unsuitable containers being used. All ashtrays should be emptied daily into a metal waste bin provided with a metal lid and taken outside. It is dangerous to empty ashtrays into plastic waste sacks, which are then left inside for disposal at a later time.

The smoking area(s) should be kept clear of combustibles and any furniture should be maintained in good repair.

[12] Further guidance has been issued by the HSE.

1.7 Managing building work and alterations

Many animal establishments and riding stables will include a mixture of both temporary and permanent buildings and structures.

Fires are more frequent when buildings are undergoing maintenance, refurbishment or alteration.

You should ensure that, before any work starts, you have evaluated the fire risks or reviewed the fire risk assessment as appropriate and have considered what dangers are likely to be introduced.

You will need to evaluate the risks to people (and animals), particularly in those areas that continue to be occupied. While alterations take place, lack of pre-planning can lead to haphazard co-ordination of fire safety measures.

Additional risks that can occur during building work include:

- hot work, including plumbing, welding or paint stripping;

- temporary electrical equipment;

- blocking of escape routes, including external escape routes;

- loss of normal storage facilities or reduced capacity;

- fire safety equipment, such as automatic fire/smoke detection systems, becoming affected;

- fire-resisting partitions being breached or fire-resisting self-closing doors wedged or held in the open position;[13] and

- additional personnel, staff, visitors and contractors who may be unfamiliar with the animal buildings.

You should liaise and exchange information with all contractors, who will also have a duty under separate legislation[14] to carry out a risk assessment and inform you of their significant findings and the preventive measures they may employ. The contractors' agreed work method statement might support this.

You should continuously monitor the impact of the building work on the general fire safety precautions, such as the increased risk from quantities of combustible materials and accumulated waste. You should only allow the minimum materials necessary for the work in hand within or adjacent to any of your stable buildings.

You must notify the fire and rescue service about alterations in your premises if an alterations notice is in force.

Further guidance on fire safety during construction work is given by the HSE and the Fire Protection Association.

1.8 The farrier

Very few stables or equine centres will have their own purpose-built blacksmith's shop for the farrier to carry out their operations.

Where the farrier is peripatetic and works for you and other stables, the fire risk assessment and the fire safety management of the stables should identify a fixed location for the farrier to work. For small stables the location may be in the open air adjacent to the individual horse stalls.

If the farrier is required to work in a suitable building under cover, the floor should be non-combustible and clear of all combustible waste materials. Using a barn, which is full of hay or straw, for the farrier's hot shoeing presents a significant fire risk.

1.9 Existing layout and construction

In many animal premises, the design is for open-plan stalls and circulation areas, allowing the animals and staff to move freely throughout the building's floor areas.

Traditionally, occupants have always been advised to shut doors when fleeing from a fire, but in open-plan stable areas this may not be possible. In these open-plan areas, the fire, and especially the smoke, may spread faster to all parts of the building than expected.

You should evaluate the construction of your stables and associated buildings. This does not mean a structural survey, unless you suspect that the structure is damaged or any structural

---

[13] See Appendix C1 for information on fire-resisting separation.
[14] Construction (Health, Safety and Welfare) Regulations 1996.

fire protection is missing or damaged, but rather an informed look around to see if there are any holes and openings in floors, walls and ceilings through which smoke and fire will spread easily.

In most cases these types of buildings will have numerous natural ventilation openings to dissipate limited quantities of smoke.

Most animal premises follow the same pattern and construction as traditional agricultural buildings. A high percentage will have been constructed of timber, and many will have been treated with flammable wood preservatives over the years.

In general, older animal buildings will have more void areas, possibly hidden from view, which will allow smoke and fire to spread away from its source. Whatever your type of building, you may need to consider some of the following:

- vertical shafts, such as lifts, open stairways, or holes for moving stock around;

- false ceilings, especially if they are not fire-stopped above walls;

- voids behind wall dividers and panelling;

- unsealed holes in walls and ceilings where pipe work, cables or other services have been installed; and

- doors, particularly to stairways, which are ill-fitting or routinely left open.

1.10 Particular hazards found between stalls and in gangways, isles, corridors and stairways used as escape routes for people and animals

Items that incorporate a source of fuel, pose an ignition risk, or are sufficiently combustible to increase the fire loading should not be located in any corridor, isle, gangway or stairway that will be used as an emergency escape and animal release route.

Such items include:

- portable heaters, e.g. LPG or electric radiant heaters and electric convectors or boilers;

- gas cylinders for supplying heaters;

- cooking appliances;

- upholstered furniture;

- coat racks;

- hay bales or baskets;

- some gas pipes, meters, taps and other fittings;

- vending machines; and

- electrical equipment, such as photocopiers, blanket dryers or tack drying or cleaning equipment.

It is not unusual for small quantities of baled or loose bedding or fodder to be placed in either the gangways or isles adjacent to the stalls or placed next to the building's exit doors, thereby reducing the circulation widths and floor areas for people and animals to exit the building in an emergency.

However, depending on the findings of your risk assessment, some of the above items may be acceptable, e.g. if there is an alternative escape route and minimum exit widths are maintained. Minimum exit door widths for leading horses out of the building are greater than the single exit door width for people to exit the building.

1.11 Combustible insulated core panels

Some of the more modern stable buildings have insulated core panels as exterior cladding or for internal upper structures and partitions (excluding the animal areas). Those animal establishments that provide residential accommodation also use insulated, soundproof core panels, mainly due to the ease of construction. This enables alterations and additional internal partitioning to take place with the minimum disruption to the operation of the business.

Panels normally consist of a central insulated core, sandwiched between an inner and outer metal skin. The central core can be made of various insulating materials, ranging from virtually non-combustible through to highly combustible.

Figure 16: Insulated core panels – internal panel

There has been an increase in serious fires in premises that has highlighted particular dangers associated with insulated core panel construction. Normally, it is the activities carried out within a building or the contents of a building that mainly contribute to the spread of fire. However, with insulated core panels the fabric of the building can also be a source of fuel and contribute to the fire.

The following measures will help to reduce any additional risk that may be generated by using insulated core panels:

• Do not store highly combustible materials (hay or straw) or install heating appliances against the panels. Control all ignition sources that are adjacent to or are required to penetrate the panels.

• Repair damaged panels and sealed joints immediately and make sure that jointing compounds or gaskets used around the edges of the panels are in good order.

• Check that where openings have been made for doors, windows, cables and ducts, they have been effectively sealed with fire-resisting sealants and the inner core has not been exposed.

• Ensure that there has been no mechanical damage, e.g. caused by forklift trucks, rough handling of stock or allowing animals near the panels.

• Ensure that panels supporting loads, such as storage areas for equipment, have been designed and installed to perform this function.

A competent person should install such construction in accordance with industry guidance. The use of such panels in areas of buildings with a high human and animal life risk, e.g. where large numbers of people or animals are present, should warrant particular consideration given the increased fire loading and rapid fire and smoke development associated with such construction.

Your fire risk assessment may need to be revised to ensure that any increased risk resulting from this type of construction is considered.[15]

1.12 Restricting the spread of fire and smoke

To reduce the risk to people and animals in the event of fire, you need to consider how to control or restrict the spread of fire and smoke throughout any building.

Smoke and gases overcome the majority of people and animals who die in fires. To evaluate the risk in your premises you must have a basic appreciation of the way fires grow and how smoke and poisonous gases can spread through buildings. A fire in an animal building with modern fittings and materials generates smoke that is thick and black, obscures vision, causes great difficulty in breathing and can block the escape routes.

Older buildings, many of which are former agricultural buildings, were deliberately constructed with holes in the brickwork to ensure cross-flow natural ventilation, thereby enabling the spread of smoke to other parts of the premises. Modern buildings following the building regulations and the British Standard for agricultural buildings make little reference to restricting the spread of fire and smoke. Ideally, buildings in excess of 25m in length should be divided up into floor-to-ceiling compartments to prevent fire and smoke travelling the entire length of the building and involving all the animals.

Fire-resisting structures
Many animal buildings can be divided into different areas or compartments by fire-resisting doors, walls and floors. These are

---

[15] See Appendix E for information on core panels in cold food storage.

partly designed to keep a fire within one area, giving people more time to escape. You will need to identify which doors, walls and floors in your buildings are fire-resisting. There may be information available from when the building was built, if alterations have been made, or from a previously held fire certificate or building regulations approval.

Normally, if there are fire-resisting doors in a wall then the wall itself will also need to be fire-resisting.[16] If you decide that a wall or floor is of fire-resisting construction, then you should not make any holes in it, e.g. for extra doors, pipe or cable ducts, without consulting a competent person.

Tents and marquees

Marquees and large tents are common at animal establishments holding special events where large numbers of people and animals are present. The following information is provided to assist you in managing the fire risk.

Modern fabrics are generally fire-retardant. However, special criteria may apply to tents and marquees, particularly where high occupancy levels are expected. All fabrics should meet an appropriate fire performance standard (further guidance can be found in BS 7837-8). Materials that are durable or non-durable may be adversely affected by weathering, so fabric that has achieved the required level of flame retardancy by chemical treatment will need to be periodically retreated.

If the tent or marquee is in constant use throughout the summer season, such retreating should be carried out when the fabric is showing signs of obvious wear or aging and not later than five years after the date when the panel was made up. Thereafter, testing should be carried out at two-yearly intervals. Such test results should be suitably certified.

Air supported structures should comply with the recommendations given in BS 6661.[17]

Pneumatic structures

A risk peculiar to pneumatic structures is that their stability is dependent upon a supply of air under pressure, which is provided and maintained by mechanical fans. Additionally such structures comprise extensive areas of flexible membrane material, which, like those used for tents, requires particular care in selection.

For these reasons, safety measures peculiar to pneumatic structures include reliability of air supply systems supplemented by secondary support systems to maintain clear exit routes in case of collapse together with the selection of suitable (flame-retarded) membrane materials. The membrane of an air supported structure should not readily support combustion. Experience has shown that PVC coated polyesters and polyamides and unreinforced polythene generally perform satisfactorily under fire conditions. A small number of fire tests on air supported structures of various sizes have shown that if the flames in a fire reach and damage the membranes at a high level (above 2.5m), the internal pressure will be reduced and, depending on the size of the hole, the fan capacity and the number of doors opened, the structure may collapse.

Combustible contents

Most enclosures (marquees, temporary building etc.) at your event or venue will contain a range of combustible contents. All materials used in finishing and furnishing should, as far as reasonably practicable, be difficult to ignite and provide a low surface spread of flame and low rates of heat release and smoke emission.

Combustible contents are likely to include:

- furnishings, upholstered seating, furniture and cushions;

- curtains, drapes and other textile hangings;

- artificial and dried foliage;

- decorative textile fabrics (e.g. within stands);

- sports and play area furnishings, such as cellular foam gym mats; and

- scenery or properties used for stage presentations.

The use of furnishings and other materials which are easily ignited or have rapid spread of flame characteristics should be avoided.

All fabrics, curtains, drapes and similar features should either be non-combustible or be of durably or inherently flame retardant fabric. Upholstered seating, carpets and other textile

---

[16] Appendix C gives further information about fire-resisting walls.
[17] See Appendix E.

floor coverings should be resistant to ignition. Foam for props and similar equipment should ideally contain only combustion modified high resilience foam.

Scenery used for stage presentations often comprise combustible materials, so you need to take particular care with their use. In particular, when they are on an open stage area within an enclosure, when you should seek to use only materials which you know are not combustible.

Ad-hoc flame tests
Ad-hoc flame tests can be used on a small sample to screen out some materials. Simple match tests, or using a cigarette lighter on a small sample, can be used to assess ease of ignition, provided that the test is carried out in the open air, away from combustible materials and with a fire extinguisher to hand.

Smoke ventilation
In larger stable buildings there may be some form of cross-flow natural or automatic smoke ventilation provided for the safety of the occupants. This is designed to restrict the spread of fire and smoke by venting the heat and smoke up through the roof or via natural openings to the outside.

Specially designed down-stands may have been installed to create a reservoir, which will contain the smoke and hot gases at ceiling or roof level, while louvers or vents allow the smoke to escape.

In smaller stables and associated buildings, either purpose-built or converted former farm buildings, ventilation will be created by either natural openings or structural alterations carried out over the years.

It is important to understand that any smoke can and will flow easily into the reservoirs and that nothing that could cause an obstruction, e.g. bales of fodder, bedding, unwanted items of tack or equipment, must be positioned near the louvers, vents or openings.

In large stables or barns, the front of individual buildings often forms part of the smoke control design. If your building has purpose-built smoke vents fitted or any other form of smoke control, then you may need to seek advice from someone who is competent in such arrangements.

[18] Communities and Local Government, 2003, *Fire Statistics UK, 2001*

1.13 Arson

Recent studies indicate that over 3,500 deliberately set fires which resulted in deaths, occur virtually every week. In equine premises it is estimated that 75% of all fires are deliberately set. All animal premises can be targeted either deliberately or just because they offer easy access.

Be aware of other small, deliberately set fires in the locality, as this can indicate an increased risk to your premises. Be suspicious of any small 'accidental' fires in the area on equine premises. You should investigate the reason for them fully.

Fires started deliberately can be particularly dangerous because they generally develop much faster and may be intentionally started in escape routes, tack rooms and the animals' accommodation. Of all the risk-reduction measures, the most benefit may come from efforts to reduce the threat from arson.

Measures to reduce arson may include:

- ensuring that the outside of the premises is constantly and well lit and, if practical, securing the perimeter of the premises and yard;

- securing all the entry points into the premises, including all the windows and the roof openings (but you must make sure that any people working late or alone still have adequate escape routes);

- making sure you regularly remove all combustible rubbish away from buildings;

- making sure that all manure heaps are at least 25m away from buildings, preferably downwind of the stables;

- not placing rubbish skips adjacent to buildings and securing waste wheelie bins in a compound separated from all the buildings;

- encouraging staff to challenge people acting suspiciously;

- removing automatic entry rights from staff who have been dismissed;

- ensuring that your security alarm/fire warning systems are monitored and acted upon;

- securing flammable liquids and gases so that intruders cannot use them;

- parking vehicles in either a garage or a secure compound; and

- fitting secure metal letterboxes on the inside of letter flaps to contain any burning materials that may be pushed through.

The British Horse Society's publication *Guidance for Fire Safety in Equine and Agricultural Premises* has a comprehensive arson risk assessment form.

The Arson Prevention Bureau has published further guidance on reducing the risk of arson, but not specifically for the equine industry.[19]

1.14 People especially at risk at your stables

Of all the people who may be especially at risk, you will need to pay particular attention to those people who have some form of impairment or disability. The Disability Rights Commission estimates that 11 million people in this country have some form of disability. This may impact on their ability to leave any building in the event of a fire. Under the Disability Discrimination Act (1995), if disabled people could realistically expect to use the service you provide at your animal premises then you must anticipate any reasonable adjustments that would make it easier for that right to be exercised.

Accordingly, if disabled people are going to be on your premises then you must also provide a safe means for them to leave if a fire occurs.

The majority of disabled people wish to and are able to facilitate their own escape. When disabled people such as employees, volunteers or livery owners use the premises, their needs should be discussed with them. These will often be modest and may require only changes or modifications to existing procedures.

In premises with a simple layout or small stables, all staff should be aware that disabled people may not react, or can react differently, to a fire warning or fire. In most cases, a common sense approach will suffice, such as offering to help lead a blind person or assisting an elderly person down steps.

The Disability Discrimination Act (1995) includes the concept of 'reasonable adjustments' and this can be carried over into fire safety law. It can mean different things in different circumstances. For a small business it may be considered reasonable to provide contrasting colours on a handrail to help people with vision impairment follow an escape route more easily. However, it might be unreasonable to expect that same business to install an expensive voice alarm system. Appropriate 'reasonable adjustments' for a large business or organisation may be much more significant.

The needs of people with mental disabilities or spatial recognition problems should be considered. The range of disabilities encountered can be considerable, extending from mild epilepsy to complete disorientation in an emergency situation. Many of these can be addressed by discrete and empathetic use of the 'buddy system' or by careful planning of colour schemes, such as nominating stairs as 'blue stairs' or 'red stairs'.

Disabled employees and other disabled people who frequently use a building may need to develop an individual 'personal emergency evacuation plan' (PEEP). If members of the public use your building then you may need to develop a range of standard PEEPs, which can be provided on request to a disabled person.

Guidance on removing barriers to the everyday needs of disabled people is contained in BS 8300. Much of this advice will also assist disabled people during an evacuation.*

---

[19] See www.arsonpreventionbureau.org.uk for further information.

* Further guidance can be found in Supplementary Guide – means of escape for disabled people, available at www.communities.gov.uk/fire and further advice can be obtained from the Disability Rights Commission at www.drc-gb.org

1.15 Vehicles

During dry conditions, additional precautions may be necessary to prevent the spread of fire to permanent or temporary structures through the ignition of vegetation by vehicles. Ensure that all vegetation is kept short to prevent contact with the engine's hot exhaust system. Particular attention is drawn to the practice of parking vehicles in stubble fields adjacent to the animal buildings.

Whenever possible, vehicle parking should be separate from any event. Vehicle movements must be controlled before, during and after any event. Catering facilities and operations involving vehicles and trailers present additional risks and should be assessed in detail. Further guidance on the measures to be taken can be found in the *Open air events and venues* guide.*

*Available at www.communities.gov.uk/fire.

Section 2 Further guidance on fire detection and warning systems

2.1 Simple fire warning arrangements

While the fire risk assessment identifies that there is a need for the animal establishment to have some form of fire warning arrangement, it may not justify the need for an expensive electrical fire warning system to be provided.

Simple hand-operated fire warning arrangements could include:

- a rotary gong;
- a triangle;
- a hand-operated bell;
- a klaxon or hand-operated siren; or
- a simple self-contained, battery operated call point and sounder.

All the above arrangements should be capable of being heard in all parts of the stable yard and paddocks and inside all the buildings.

Note: Audible fire warning facilities may have adverse effects on the animals' behaviour.

Where an electrical fire warning system is considered necessary, then a straightforward arrangement typically includes the following:

- a simple control and indicator panel; and
- electronic sirens or bells.

An alternative system of interconnected combined manual call points and sounders may be equally acceptable.

If your building has areas where a fire could develop undetected or where people work alone and might not see a fire immediately, then it may be necessary to upgrade your fire warning system to incorporate suitable automatic fire detection or to install an automatic fire detection and warning system.

If, for any reason, your system fails, you must still ensure that all people at your stables can be warned and escape safely. A temporary arrangement, such as whistles or air horns, combined with suitable training, may be acceptable for a very short period.

The fire warning sound levels should be such that everyone is alerted, taking into account background noise. In areas with high ambient noise levels or where people may be wearing ear protectors, the audible warning should be supplemented, e.g. with visual alarms.

Special considerations will need to be paid to those buildings where animals are present as the traditional audible sounders will most likely disturb the animals, making it difficult to release them from their stalls or the building.

Visual warning indicators with a buzzer or other suitable sounder should be installed to attract the staff's attention. This staff warning arrangement will also need to be used to attract the staff's and other people's attention when outside in the yard areas.

Research has shown that some people, and in particular members of the public, do not always react quickly to a conventional fire alarm. Voice alarms are therefore becoming increasingly popular and can also incorporate a public address facility. However, it is essential to ensure that voice alarm systems are designed and installed by a person with specialist knowledge of these systems, especially in stables and livery yards.

Consideration should also be given to the provision of a schematic plan showing fire alarm zones in a multi-zoned system. This should be displayed adjacent to the fire alarm control panel.

People with hearing difficulties

Where people have hearing difficulties, particularly those who are profoundly deaf, then simply hearing the fire warning is likely to be the major difficulty. If these people are never alone while on the premises then this may not be a serious problem, as it would be reasonable for other occupants to provide an indication that the building should be evacuated. If a person with hearing difficulties is likely to be alone, then other means of raising the alarm should be considered. Among the most popular are visual beacons and/or pagers that are linked to the existing fire alarm.

2.2 Manual call points

Manual call points, often known as 'break-glass' call points, enable a person who discovers a fire to immediately raise the alarm and warn other people in the stables of the danger.

Break-glass call points are not recommended for buildings containing animals; frangible call points should be used in all areas where animals are likely to be present.

People leaving a building because of a fire will use the nearest available way out, whether it is a normal door, a roller shutter or a fire exit. Consequently, manual call points are normally positioned on each floor at every exit and storey exit, not just those designated as fire exits.

Manual call points should normally be positioned so that, after all fixtures and fittings, machinery and stock are in place, no one should have to travel more than 45m to the nearest alarm point. This distance may be less if your premises cater for people of limited mobility, or there are animals or particularly hazardous areas. They should be conspicuous, fitted at a height of about 1.4m (or less for premises with a significant number of wheelchair users), and not in an area likely to be obstructed.

Detailed guidance on manual call points is given in British Standard EN54-11.*

2.3 Automatic fire detection

Automatic fire detection will normally only be required under fire safety law when it is needed to safeguard life, for example:

- if a fire can trap people who are isolated or in remote areas, such as lone workers, and they could become trapped because they are unaware of its development;

- as a compensating feature, e.g. for inadequate structural fire protection, in dead-ends or where there are extended travel distances; and

- where the building's smoke control and ventilation systems are controlled by the automatic fire detection system.

Automatic fire detection is often installed for the protection of animals and property as part of the animal premises' business continuity or damage limitation arrangements.

Providing traditional automatic fire detection equipment in buildings providing animal accommodation or the storage of bedding and fodder is not normally successful due to the potential for false alarms associated with dusty atmospheres, cobwebs, insects or steam from the animals. The most suitable detection system will be an optical single-point beam positioned at the highest point of the open ceiling area. This can be programmed to ignore bats and birds that may get into the building.

Stables and other animal establishments that provide onsite residential accommodation for staff and members of the public should refer to standards for automatic detection set out in the separate guide for sleeping accommodation.

Your specialist fire alarm engineer will advise you of the most suitable equipment and positioning.

2.4 Staff alarms, voice evacuation and public address systems

Research has shown that some people, and in particular members of the public, do not always react quickly to a conventional fire alarm at large events in the open air, including animal establishments such as stables and livery yards. Public address (PA) and voice evacuation systems are therefore very important at these events, activities and establishments as they give staff, the public and visitors explicit information about the emergency or about action they are required to take.

A message or messages can be relayed to many people at the same time but you must consider what information to provide, and how to communicate it succinctly. The announcer should have a good view over as much of the stables and yards as possible and effective communication links with all the buildings at the establishment.

*See Appendix E: References.

It is important to establish the required levels of audibility and speech clarity for the system. It is therefore essential to ensure that the public address and voice alarm systems are designed and installed by a person with specialist knowledge of these installations.

Guidance on voice alarm systems can be found in BS 5839-8, *Guidance on sound systems used for emergency purpose*, and BS EN 60849.

2.5 Reducing false alarms

False alarms from automatic fire detection systems are a major problem and result in over 280,000 unwanted calls to the fire and rescue service every year.[20]

If there are excessive false alarms in your premises, people may become complacent and not respond correctly to a warning of a real fire. In such circumstances, you may be failing to comply with fire safety law. As a rule of thumb, an acceptable rate of false alarms is less than one per 50 detectors per 12-month period. If it appears that the rate of false alarms is likely to exceed this, then a competent person should carry out a special investigation of the cause.

To reduce the number of false alarms, a review of the system design and location of detection and activation devices should be undertaken. For example, if a smoke detector is positioned in a staff canteen with cooking facilities then the likelihood of the detector being set off is increased. Similarly, if a manual call point is positioned in a stock area where there is continual movement of stock, the call point is likely to be accidentally damaged. In this case a simple, fabricated metal cage around the call point is likely to solve the problem.

Occasionally, people set off a manual call point in the genuine but incorrect belief that there is a fire. Nothing should be done to discourage such actions and the number of false alarms generated this way is not significant.

Further detailed guidance on reducing false alarms is available in BS 5839-1.[21]

---

[20] Communities and Local Government, 2004, *Fire Statistics UK, 2002*.
[21] Guidance on reducing false alarms has been published by DCLG/CACFOA/BFPSA. See Appendix E: References.

Note: Due to the fire service's efforts to reduce expenditure arising from attending false alarms, you should check with your local fire brigade as to whether they would attend your animal premises before you have carried out a thorough search to ascertain the origin of the alarm. This is particularly relevant for stables that have connected their fire warning system to a remote monitoring centre, which then passes the call on to the fire brigade.

2.6 Staged fire alarms

In the majority of animal premises, the actuation of the fire warning system should trigger the immediate and total evacuation of all the buildings. However, in some large or complex animal premises this may not be necessary as alternative arrangements should be in place.

These alternative arrangements broadly fall into two groups. Firstly, those people potentially most at risk from a fire, usually those closest to where the alarm was activated, will be immediately evacuated, while others in other areas of the premises are given an alert signal and will only evacuate should it become necessary. This is generally termed a phased evacuation, and the initial movement, depending on the layout and configuration of the premises, can be either horizontal or vertical.

The second alternative is for the initial alert signal to be given to occupants, or more commonly to certain staff, who then carry out pre-arranged actions to assist others to evacuate more easily. It requires able, fully trained staff to be available at all times and should not be seen as a simple means of reducing disruption to working practices. Where a staged evacuation strategy is in place, disabled people should be alerted at the first stage to maximise their potential escape time.

In animal establishments that provide sleeping accommodation for staff and/or members of the public, the initial actuation of the fire alarm system should alert and start the evacuation of all people.

These arrangements require fire warning systems capable of giving staged alarms, including an 'alert signal' and a different 'evacuate signal', and should only be considered after consultation with specialist installers and, if necessary, the relevant enforcing authority.

Such systems also require a greater degree of management to ensure that staff and others are familiar with the procedures, systems and actions required.

2.7 Testing and maintenance

A named responsible person should supervise your fire warning and detection systems. They should be given sufficient authority and training to manage all aspects of the routine testing and scrutiny of the systems.

The control and indicating equipment should be checked at least every 24 hours to ensure there are no specific faults indicated. All types of fire warning system should be tested once a week. For electrical systems, a manual call point should be activated (using a different call point for each successive test), usually by inserting a dedicated test key. This will check that the control equipment is capable of receiving a signal and, in turn, activating the warning alarms. Manual call points may be numbered to ensure that they are tested sequentially.

Figure 17: A test key

It is good practice to test the alarm at the same time each week, but additional tests may be required to ensure that staff or people present outside normal working hours are given the opportunity to hear the alarm.

Systems that are connected to a central monitoring station must be taken off watch for the duration of the test.

A competent person with specialist knowledge of fire warning and automatic detection systems should carry out six-monthly servicing and preventive maintenance. Entering into a service contract with a specialist fire alarm company normally fulfils this task.[22]

As part of the stable management's responsibilities, it is good practice to record all tests and false alarms and any maintenance carried out.

2.8 Guaranteed power supply

If your fire risk assessment concludes that an electrical fire warning system is necessary, then the British Standard BS 5839-1:2002 requires it to have a back-up power supply.

Whatever back-up system is used, it should normally be capable of operating the fire warning and detection system for a minimum period of 24 hours and sounding the alarm signal in all areas for 30 minutes.

2.9 Appropriate standards

New systems and those undergoing substantial alterations should normally comply with the recommendations of the appropriate part of BS 5839. If you are unsure whether your existing system is adequate, you will need to consult a competent person.

---

[22] See the reference to third party certification schemes in Step 3.4.6.

Section 3 Further guidance on firefighting equipment and facilities

All animal establishments, stables and livery yards should be provided with appropriate firefighting equipment. For the majority of premises and buildings, first aid firefighting equipment (portable extinguishers) should be sufficient. However, in large and more complex buildings at your animal establishment, you may need to consider providing some form of fixed firefighting equipment in the form of water mist and/or fire hydrants, with any associated equipment.

Figure 18: Provision of firefighting equipment

The type(s) of firefighting equipment will vary according to local conditions and the risks to be covered. For example, there may need to be firefighting equipment for tackling fires in parked vehicles, manure heaps and refuse storage facilities, vegetation areas, etc. An effective arrangement is to provide well indicated fire points as detailed below.

3.1 Portable firefighting equipment

Firefighting equipment appropriate to the specific risks found at your stables should be provided in accordance with Table 3 below. Before looking at the different types of extinguisher, it is important to consider the variety of combustible material in your premises that may be involved in a fire.

It must be appreciated that for very small stables and yards, the provision of firefighting equipment does not necessarily mean providing the traditional expensive fire extinguishers one would normally expect in high street offices or shops.

Fires generated by different materials are classed as follows.

Table 3: Class of fire

Class of fire	Description
Class A	Fires involving solid materials such as hay, straw, wood shavings, paper, cardboard or textiles.
Class B	Fires involving flammable liquids such as petrol or diesel fuel oils.
Class C	Fires involving gases.
Class D	Fires involving metals (unlikely to be found at stables, other than in vehicle components).
Class F	Fires involving cooking oils such as in kitchens with deep-fat fryers.

If there is a possibility of fires at your premises involving materials in the shaded boxes in the above table, then you should seek advice from a competent person.

Number and type of extinguishers

In some smaller animal premises, multi-purpose extinguishers **(but not dry powder)**, which can cover a range of risks, may be appropriate. These may be obtained from local retail outlets or from specialist suppliers.

Generally, at least one water-based extinguisher for approximately every 200m² of indoor floor space, with a minimum of two extinguishers per floor, will be adequate. Depending on the outcome of your fire risk assessment, it may be possible to reduce this to one extinguisher in very small stables with a floor space of less than 90m².

You should position the fire extinguishers on escape routes, close to the exit doors from the stables, room or floor, the final exit from the building, or, if necessary, adjacent to any special hazard.

They should be placed on a dedicated stand or hung on a wall at a convenient height so that employees can easily lift them off (about 1m for larger extinguishers, 1.5m for smaller ones). Ideally no one should have to travel more than 30m to reach a fire extinguisher.

Consideration should be given to the implications of the Manual Handling Regulations when selecting and siting firefighting equipment.

Firefighting equipment positioned on the outside of buildings must be protected against the weather and extreme temperatures.

Firefighting equipment positioned within dusty environments, i.e. stables and bedding or fodder storage buildings, must be covered to prevent dust coating the extinguisher and entering the operating and discharge points.

Protective covers or weatherproof enclosures must be marked with suitable signage indicating the location of the firefighting equipment.

Extinguishers manufactured to current standards should be predominately red and may have a colour-coded area, sited above or within the instructions, denoting the type of extinguisher (see the colours below). Older extinguishers will have been manufactured with the body of the extinguisher painted entirely in a single colour. These older extinguishers remain acceptable until they are no longer serviceable.

However, it is good practice to ensure that old and new style extinguishers are not mixed on the same floor of a building. Where old and new types are put together, staff must be trained to recognise and use the types and styles of fire extinguishers.

The most common types of firefighting equipment, their range, capabilities and relevant colour codes are described below.

Note: Fire extinguishers that when operated produce a loud noise, e.g. CO_2, or large clouds of dry powder, **should not** be used in close proximity to animals.

Figure 19: Types of fire extinguishers

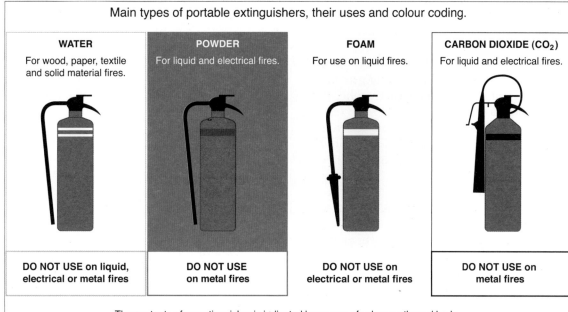

Old style colour coding of fire extinguishers

Water extinguishers (red)
This type of extinguisher can only be used on Class A fires. They allow the user to direct water onto a fire from a considerable distance. A 9-litre water extinguisher can be quite heavy and some of the water extinguishers with additives described below can achieve the same rating although they are smaller and therefore considerably lighter. This type of extinguisher is not suitable for use where 240-volt or 415-volt live electrical equipment is involved.

Water extinguishers with additives (red)
This type of extinguisher is suitable for Class A fires. They can also be suitable for use on Class B fires and, where appropriate, this will be indicated on the extinguisher. They are generally more efficient than conventional water extinguishers.

Water-based extinguishers with additives have been found to be more effective on fires involving loose stacked hay and straw.

Foam extinguishers (cream)
This type of extinguisher can be used on Class A or B fires and is particularly suited to extinguishing liquid fires such as petrol or diesel. They should not be used on free-flowing liquid fires unless the operator has been specially trained, as these have the potential to rapidly spread the fire to adjacent material. This type of extinguisher is not really suitable for deep-fat fryers or chip pans.

Powder extinguishers (blue)
This type of extinguisher can be used on most classes of fire and will achieve a good 'knock down' of the fire. They can be used on fires involving electrical equipment but will almost certainly render the equipment useless. Because they do not cool the fire appreciably it can reignite.

This type of extinguisher would knock down a small fire in hay or straw, but it can drive the fire further into the pile with the potential for the fire to flare up.

Powder-type fire extinguishers **should not** be positioned in animal accommodation buildings and they **should not** be used in close proximity to animals. The dry powder can affect the animal and human respiratory systems.

Carbon dioxide extinguishers (black)
This type of extinguisher is particularly suitable for fires involving electrical equipment, as they will extinguish a fire without causing any further damage to the equipment. As with all fires involving electrical equipment, the power should be switched off or disconnected if possible. The loud noise accompanying discharge and the freezing effect on the horn of these extinguishers can cause operators to become startled and drop the extinguisher. The noise accompanying the discharge will also startle any animals nearby.

Class 'AFFF' extinguishers (yellow)

This type of extinguisher is particularly suitable for commercial catering establishments with deep-fat fryers, chip pans and electrical catering equipment.

Maintenance of portable fire extinguishers

All portable fire extinguishers will require periodic inspection, maintenance and testing. This will be dependant on local conditions, such as the likelihood of vandalism, dust or the environment. Brief checks to ensure that they remain serviceable will need to be undertaken. In normal conditions, a monthly check should suffice. Maintenance by a competent person should be carried out annually.

All checks, visual or otherwise, should be recorded in the premises' fire logbook.

Appropriate standards

The selection, installation and maintenance of fire extinguishers should comply with the appropriate part of BS 5306.[23] The colour coding of fire extinguishers should comply with BS 7863.

Fire blankets

Fire blankets should be positioned in kitchens and all locations where live flame is likely to be present, i.e. the farrier's working area where hot shoeing is carried out, where contractors are using live flame in maintenance work, etc.

Fire blankets should be hung on a wall at about 1.6m above floor level.

3.2 Fixed firefighting installations and fire points

These are firefighting systems that are normally installed within the structure of the stables.

They may already be provided in your premises or you may be considering them as a means of protecting the animals or some particular critical risk as part of your business protection or risk reduction strategy.

Selecting suitable fixed firefighting or fire-controlling systems for the protection of the animals will need careful understanding and consideration; a specialist will need to be brought in to advise you.

Hose reels

Permanent hose reels installed in accordance with the relevant British Standard[24] provide an effective firefighting capability for Class A risks. They may offer an alternative, or an addition, to portable firefighting equipment. A concern is that untrained people will stay and fight a fire when escape is the safest option. Where hose reels are installed, and your fire risk assessment expects staff to use them in the initial stages of a fire, staff should receive appropriate training. Visual checks for leaks and obvious damage should be carried out regularly and a competent person should carry out more formal maintenance checks at least annually.

When considering fire hose reels, you should ensure that, if they are positioned outside buildings, they are protected against the weather and extremes in temperature.

If sited inside buildings with dusty environments, they should be suitably enclosed to protect them from dust. The enclosure should be suitably marked to indicate the presence of the fire hose reel.

Smaller stables may need only one hose reel, providing that it can easily reach all the buildings associated with the stables. The water supply and pressure to the fire hose reel should be sufficient to provide a continuous supply and a jet of water of at least 5m throw.

When considering the use of hose reels, you should not have to take them through doorways; fire doors held open by a hose reel will also permit smoke to pass through them.

---

[23] See Appendix E for references for BS 5306-8, *Selection and installation of portable fire extinguishers*, and BS 5306-3, *Code of practice for the inspection and maintenance of portable fire extinguishers*.

[24] See Appendix E for further information on BS EN 671-1.

Figure 20: Hose reel

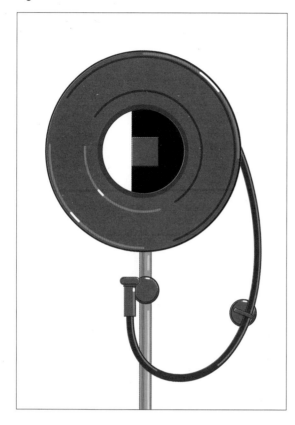

In small stables with accommodation for less than five horses, simple domestic water hoses will be considered acceptable provided they are permanently attached to the water supply, can reach all areas of the stables and yard, can supply a jet of water of not less than 5m, and are suitably protected from the weather and extreme temperatures.

Buckets and hand pumps

Where standpipes are not provided or the water pressure or flow is not sufficient, provide each fire point with a water tank of at least 250 litres in capacity fitted with a hinged lid cover, two buckets (minimum 6-litre capacity) and one hand pump or bucket pump.

The number of fire points provided will depend on the equipment provided. They should be located no more than 2m from the areas to be covered.

Sprinkler and water fog systems

Sprinkler and water fog systems can be very effective in controlling fires. These systems can be designed to protect life and property and may be regarded as a potentially cost-effective solution for reducing the risks created by fire. Sprinkler systems should normally extend to all the stable buildings, but in certain circumstances they may be acceptable in just the higher fire-loading buildings and animal life risk areas.[25]

Sprinkler and water fog systems could give additional benefits, such as a reduction in insurance premiums, a reduction in the amount of portable firefighting equipment necessary and the relaxation of restrictions in the design of animal buildings. Where installed, a sprinkler or water fog system is usually part of a package of fire precautions for a building.

The design and installation of new sprinkler systems and the maintenance of all systems should comply with the Loss Prevention Council (LPC) rules or BS EN 12845[26] and should be entrusted only to competent people.

Water fog systems have yet to receive an approved standard.

Emergency water supplies for fighting fire

A high percentage of animal premises located in rural areas will not have an adequate water supply availability to support an effective sprinkler or water fog system. Bulk storage of water accompanied by a pump to pressurise the water supply may have to be part of the fire control system, which will increase the overall cost of such installations.

Water fog systems use far less water, and for animal protection they are considered to be far more suitable than a conventional fire sprinkler system.

Routine maintenance of such installations by onsite personnel may include the checking of pressure gauges, alarm systems, water supplies, any anti-freezing devices and automatic booster pumps.

A competent maintenance contractor should provide guidance as to what records need to be completed.

If a sprinkler or water fog system forms an integral part of your fire strategy, it is imperative that adequate management procedures are in place to cater for those periods when the systems are not functional. This should form part of your emergency plan.

---

[25] See Step 3.4 for information on risk categories.
[26] BS EN 12845, *Fixed firefighting systems. Automatic sprinkler systems. Design, installation and maintenance.*

Although the actual procedures will vary, such measures may include the following:

- The system should be restored to full working order as soon as possible.

- Any planned shutdown should be limited to low risk periods when numbers of people are at a minimum (e.g. at night).

- The area without the benefit of working sprinklers may need to be isolated from the rest of the premises by fire-resisting material/construction.

- Higher risk processes such as the farrier's hot work should be avoided or located in a controlled area.

- Extra staff should be trained and dedicated to conducting fire patrols during these activities.

- Any phased or staged evacuation strategy for people or animals may need to be suspended.

- Evacuation should be immediate and complete. Caution should be exercised as the staircase widths may have been designed for phased evacuation only.

- The procedures regarding the evacuation of any animals will have to be reviewed.

- Inform the local fire and rescue service.

If, having considered all possible measures, the risk is still unacceptable, it will be necessary to close all or part of the building.

Other fixed installations
There are a number of other fixed fire control installations suitable for animal establishments, including water mist and water deluge systems. Should your premises have a fixed firefighting system that you are unfamiliar with, advice should be sought.

Where a fixed firefighting control system forms an integral part of your fire safety strategy, it should be maintained in accordance with the relevant standard by a competent person.

3.3 Other facilities (including those for firefighters)

Building regulations and other Acts, including local Acts, may have required facilities to be provided for the safety of people in the building and to assist firefighters. The fire safety law places a duty on you to maintain such facilities in good working order and at all times.

These may include:

- access roads;

- sprinkler systems;

- smoke control/ventilation systems;

- dry or wet rising mains and firefighting inlets and outlets;

- information and communication arrangements; and

- firefighters' switches for high electrical voltage signs etc.

The Workplace (Health, Safety and Welfare) Regulations 1992 also require that systems provided for safety within a workplace be maintained.

Access for fire engines and firefighters
Buildings that have been constructed to modern building regulations or in accordance with certain local Acts will have been provided with facilities that allow fire engines to approach and park within a reasonable distance (not more than 45m) so that firefighters can use their equipment without too much difficulty.

These facilities may consist of access roads to the building, hard standing areas for fire engines and access into the building for firefighters. It is essential that where such facilities are provided they are properly maintained and available for use at all relevant times.

Routes for fire engines should have a:

- road width of not less than 3.7m;

- clear width of gates not less than 3.1m;

- clear overhead height of not less than 3.7m;

- road surface that can carry a vehicle weighing 12.5 tonnes; and

- suitable area to allow a fire engine to turn around. If a turning circle is provided, the area should have a diameter of not less than 16.8m.

Where a building is used by a number of different occupants, you will need to ensure co-operation between the various responsible people to maintain fire service access. In exceptional cases, where access is persistently obstructed, you may need to make additional arrangements.

Further details are contained in Approved Document B to the Building Regulations, which should be consulted for guidance.

You should always liaise with the local fire and rescue service to ensure that your access routes are suitable for fire engines used by the service.

Foam inlets

These special inlets are usually fitted to provide an efficient way of extinguishing a fire in a basement or other area of high risk, such as an oil-fired boiler room or plant room. In many respects the external fire and rescue service's hose connection points look the same as rising main inlet boxes, but the door should be clearly marked 'foam inlet'. The risk area should be kept clear of obstructions to allow the foam to spread into the compartment.

It is unlikely that there are many equine establishments with or requiring this type of installation.

Maintenance

All types of mains and associated valves should be maintained and tested on a regular basis by a competent person. Although there are no recommended periods between maintenance checks, it would be prudent to carry out an annual service.

Firefighters' switches

Luminous discharge lighting is used infrequently in stables and yards. Where they are provided, safety switches are normally provided to isolate high-voltage luminous signs or to cut off electrical power. In the case of existing installations, if they have been provided in accordance with previous legislation (e.g. the Local Government (Miscellaneous Provisions) Act 1982), then it is likely that they will be sufficient to comply with the Order. If this is not the case, then you may need to consult the enforcing authority regarding the suitability of their location and marking. Testing should be carried out in accordance with the manufacturer's instructions. If you have no such instructions, then a competent electrician should carry out an initial test.

Other facilities

In addition to the above, other facilities may have been installed at your premises. Your fire risk assessment, emergency plan and maintenance audit should include these. Such facilities can include:

- information signs and site plans for firefighters;

- communication systems;

- static water supplies, ponds and lakes, private hydrants, meter bypass valves and underground tanks;

- standby fire pumps, electrical generators, air pumps and hydraulic motors;

- manual/close devices for roller shutter doors in fire compartment walls; and

- water deluge, water mist and sprinkler systems.

---

[27] See Appendix A for details of a sample checklist.

Section 4 Further guidance on escape routes

4.1 General principles

Having established the current level of fire risk at your animal premises or stable, the guidance information contained in this section is intended to help you when evaluating the adequacy of all the existing fire escape routes from your stables and equine buildings. The guidance offered is based on typical solutions for animal buildings of normal fire risk. If your buildings are of a higher or lower risk, it will be necessary for you to adapt these solutions accordingly.

In considering the adequacy of the existing fire escape routes for people, you should (although it will not be a statutory requirement) include within your assessment the number and widths of the existing exit door openings to ensure that the stables' staff and firefighters can quickly, safely and effectively secure the release and rescue of all the horses.

There is no obligation to adopt any particular solution contained in this guide if you prefer to meet the relevant requirements in some other way. If you decide to adopt some alternative arrangement, it will need to achieve at least an equivalent level of fire safety.

The following sections provide information on the numbers of fire exit doors, travel distances, staircases etc for normal, able-bodied people who can escape from a building by their own unaided efforts. Owners and occupiers of animal buildings and equine establishments will need to consult further guidance on suitable fire safety standards applicable for people with special mobility or impairment needs.

Suitability of escape routes
You should ensure that all the escape routes are:

- suitable for people and horses at the same time;

- easily, safely and immediately usable at all relevant times;

- adequate for the number of people and horses likely to use them;

- generally usable without passing through doors requiring a key, complicated fastenings or code to unlock; and

- free from any obstructions, slip or trip hazards.

In multi-occupied animal establishments, the escape routes should normally be independent of other owners or occupiers, i.e. staff initially should not have to go through another owner or occupier's premises as the exit routes may be secured or obstructed. Where this is not possible then robust legal agreements should be in place to ensure their availability at all relevant times.

It will be for management to decide if people with only minor mobility needs are permitted to assist with the release and evacuation of the animals.

All doors should preferably open in the direction of escape and must do so if more than 60 people or 20 horses use them, or if they provide an exit from an area of higher fire risk, e.g. stables and stalls with large quantities of hay or straw present.

While not normally acceptable, the use of certain ladders, lift-up floor hatches, wall hatches or window exits may be suitable for a small number of able-bodied, frequently trained staff in exceptional circumstances, and then only to descend not more than 3m. These ladders, hatches, etc are not considered acceptable for locations where the public, livery owners, visitors or contractors have reason to be present.

Number of people using the indoor arenas, stables, office and retail shop, livery yards or other equine buildings
As your escape routes need to be adequate for all the people likely to use them, you will need to consider the maximum number of people, including all employees, livery owners, contractors and members of the public, who may be present at any one time. Where buildings have been subject to recent building regulations approval for use as either the

animal premises' office or a retail shop, the number and width of all the escape routes and exits will normally suffice for the anticipated maximum number of people using the buildings. In such stable buildings where the risk has changed or the buildings were constructed prior to the advent of national building regulations, it is still necessary to confirm the provision.

For the stables, the tack room, storerooms, etc, the maximum numbers of the stables' staff, volunteers, livery owners, visitors and contractors that are liable to be in the individual buildings at the same time should be known by the responsible person. For the stables' shops, the responsible person should normally be aware of the maximum number of people likely to be present from a personal knowledge of trading patterns. Similarly, there will be an appreciation of the use of the buildings by those with special needs, such as the disabled.

If you propose to make changes to the use or layout of the buildings, including the number of horses to be accommodated, which may subsequently increase the number of people, you should check the design capacity by referring to guidance given in the Building Regulations Approved Document B.

> **Case study**
>
> The function of an agricultural merchants' retail shop changes from selling large quantities and items of combustible bedding and fodder, to selling just tack and outdoor clothing, etc.
>
> While it was predominantly a bedding and fodder shop, most of the sales area was used to stock and display bales of hay and straw, bags of wood shavings, etc, so fewer customers could be accommodated in the store and only a small number of fire exits was necessary.
>
> When the shop started to sell tack, outdoor clothing and associated equine accessories, more floor space was available, which could accommodate more customers. The number and widths of exits would need to be increased.

Figure 21: Retail shop

Widths and numbers of escape routes and stairways

Once you have established the maximum number of people liable to be in each of the buildings, the next step is to calculate whether the widths of exits are sufficient. The width should be measured at the narrowest part of the exit route, normally a doorway.

An ordinary exit route that is at least 750mm wide throughout its length can accommodate up to 50 people, one that is 850mm wide up to 110 people, and an exit route that is 1,050mm wide up to 220 people. For wider exits, divide that portion of the exit width greater than 1,050mm by 5mm to give the maximum number of extra people that exit can safely accommodate.

Exit doors and routes which will be used by people and horses at the same time will need to be at least 2.4m high and not less than 1.2m wide.

When calculating the overall available exit capacity for buildings that have more than one way out, you should assume that the widest is not available due to it being compromised by fire. If several exit doors are close to one another, you should consider whether the fire could affect two or more at the same time, and if that is the case it may be necessary to discount them from your exit width calculation.

Mobility impairment

Effective management arrangements will need to be put in place for those people who will require assistance to escape.

The following points should be considered:

- Where refuges are provided, they should be enclosed in a fire-resisting structure, which leads directly to the open air or a protected escape route. They should only be used in conjunction with effective management rescue arrangements. Your fire safety strategy should not rely on the fire and rescue service rescuing people waiting in these refuges.

- Sufficient and suitable escape routes should always be available for use by disabled people. This does not mean that every exit will need to be adapted. Staff should be aware of routes suitable for disabled people so that they can direct and assist people accordingly.

- The premises' fire strategy should always be directed to assisting people with mobility needs before releasing and rescuing the animals.

Fire-resisting construction

The type and age of construction of all animal buildings are crucial factors to consider when assessing the adequacy of the existing escape routes out of the buildings. To ensure the safety of people, it may be necessary to protect escape routes from the effects of fire and smoke. In older premises[1] it is possible that the type of construction and materials used may not perform to current fire standards. Also, changes of proprietors and subsequent alterations and refurbishment may have led to:

- cavities and voids being created, allowing the potential for a fire to spread unseen;

- doors worn by age and movement being less likely to limit the spread of smoke;

- damaged or lack of cavity barriers in modular construction; and

- breaches in fire compartment walls, floors and ceilings created by the installation of new services, e.g. plumbing, heating, lighting, a fire alarm system or computer cabling.

Where it is concluded that an escape route needs to be separated from the rest of the building by fire-resisting construction, e.g. a dead-end corridor or protected staircase, then you should ensure the following:

- Doors, walls, floors and ceilings protecting fire escape routes should be capable of resisting the passage of smoke and fire for a sufficient period of time for people to escape from the building. Where suspended or false ceilings are provided, the fire resistance of the walls and partitions should extend up through the false ceiling to the floor slab level above.

- For means of escape purposes for people, a half-hour fire-resisting rating is normally sufficient. Where the release and rescue of horses from the stalls is part of the stables' fire plan, then the fire resistance, especially to floors over basements, should be increased to at least one hour.

If there is any doubt as to the nature of the construction of your premises, further advice can be sought from a competent person.

Inner rooms

Where the only way out of an inner room located inside an animal building is through the main animal stalls area, an unnoticed fire in the outer area could trap people in the inner room. This should be avoided where possible. If, however, this cannot be achieved, then sufficient early warning of a fire should be provided by any one of the following means:

- sufficient clear glazed panels between the two rooms providing adequate vision to all the floor areas of the stalls, to give an early indication of the conditions in the outer floor areas and the availability of the means of escape;

- sufficient gap between the dividing wall or partition and the ceiling of the inner room, e.g. at least 500mm, so that smoke will be quickly seen; or

- a suitable automatic smoke detector in the outer floor areas that will sound a warning in the inner room.

---

[1] Further information on listed historical properties can be found in Appendix D.

Figure 22: Inner rooms

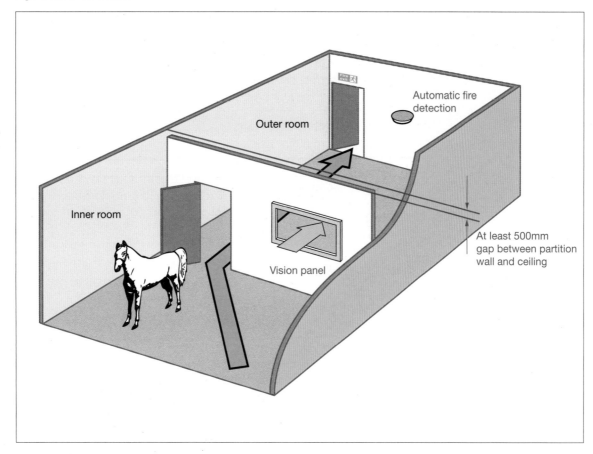

Outer room

Automatic fire detection

Inner room

Vision panel

At least 500mm gap between partition wall and ceiling

Travel distance

Having established the maximum number and the locations of people, the number of exit doors and the exit capacity required to evacuate them safely, you will now need to confirm that the number and location of the existing fire exits are adequate. In new animal buildings which have been designed and constructed in accordance with modern building standards, the travel distances will already have been calculated. Once you have completed your fire risk assessment, you will now need to confirm that those distances are still relevant.

The following table gives guidance on travel distances for people only. It should be understood, however, that these distances are flexible and may be increased or even decreased – this will depend on the level of residual fire risk after you have put in place the appropriate fire prevention measures.

For staff to release and rescue animals from their stalls, these distances should be reduced by two-thirds.

Table 2: Suggested travel distances

Escape routes	Suggested range of travel distance
Where more than one route is provided	25m in high fire risk area* 45m in normal fire risk area 60m in low fire risk area
Where only a single escape route is provided	12m in high fire risk area* 18m in normal fire risk area 25m in low fire risk area

*Where there are small 'high fire risk' areas, this travel distance should apply. Where the risk assessment indicates that the whole building is a high fire risk, advice should be sought from a competent person.

When assessing travel distances, you need to consider the distance to be travelled by people when escaping, allowing for walking around any work benches, furniture, stacks of bedding or piles or bags of fodder, feed, etc.

Note: Where the animal premises' fire procedure plans include attempts by the staff to release and rescue the horses tethered in their stalls, the numbers and widths of the exit doors will have to be increased, and travel distances to these exit doors from the stalls will need to be reduced.

The distance for people to travel to the nearest exit doors should be measured from all parts of the floor areas to the nearest place of reasonable safety, which is:

• a fire-protected staircase enclosure;

• a separate fire compartment from which there is a final exit to a place of total safety; or

• a final exit door that opens directly to the open air.

The suggested travel distances may be increased by the installation of fire protection measures, e.g. automatic smoke detection, sprinklers, water fog systems or smoke ventilation. Alternative fire exits from an open floor area or room should be located at least 45° apart, unless the routes to them are separated by fire-resistant construction (see Figure 23).

If in doubt, consult a competent person.

Figure 23: Alternative exits seperated by fire-resisting construction

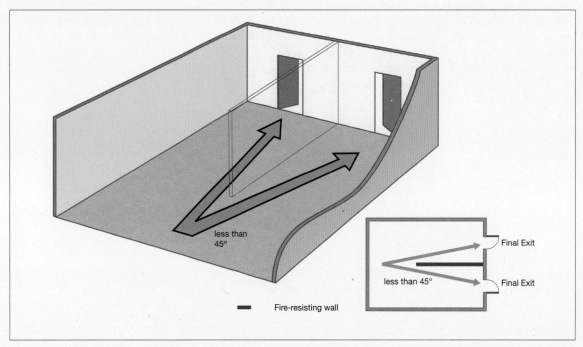

Figure 24: Measuring travel distance

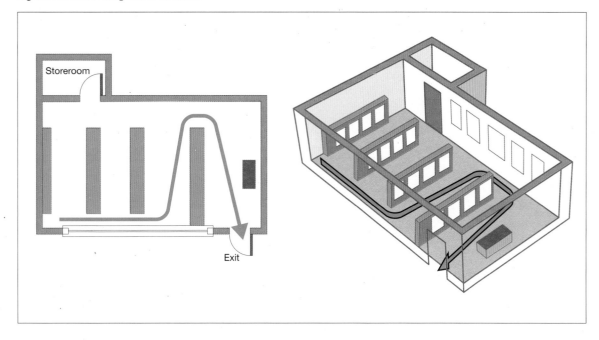

Figure 25: Alternative exits

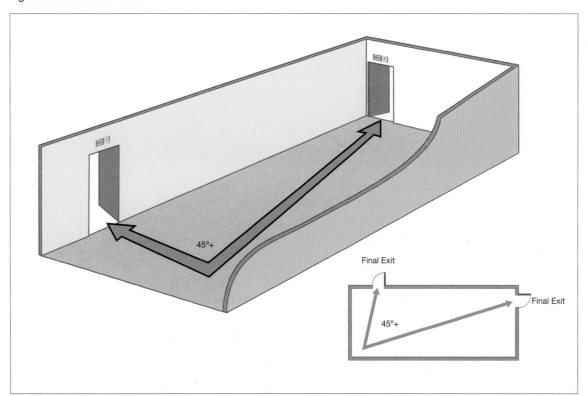

Measuring travel distances for initial dead-end travel

Where the initial direction of travel is in one direction only, this should be limited and any alternative exits should be positioned to ensure that a fire will not compromise both exits.

Figure 26: Measuring travel distance from initial dead end (open plan)

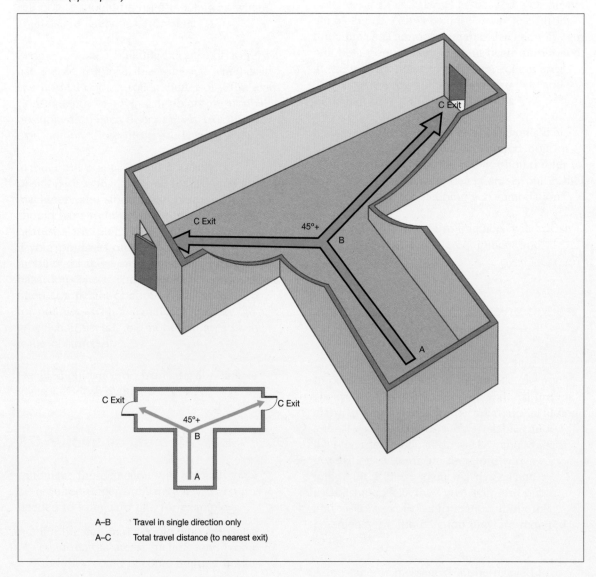

A–B   Travel in single direction only

A–C   Total travel distance (to nearest exit)

Areas with dead-end conditions

If your animal buildings have areas from which escape can be made in one direction only (a dead end), then an undetected fire in that area could affect people trying to escape. To overcome this problem, the travel distance should be limited (see Table 2) and one of the following solutions should be employed:

- An alternative exit may be provided (see Figure 28).

- The exit route may be constructed of fire-resisting partitions and self-closing doors to allow people to escape safely past a room in which a fire has occurred (see Figure 29).

- An automatic smoke detection and warning system may be installed in those areas where a fire could pose a risk to the escape route (see Figure 30).

Alternative approaches may be acceptable; however, expert advice may be necessary.

Figure 27: Dead-end condition

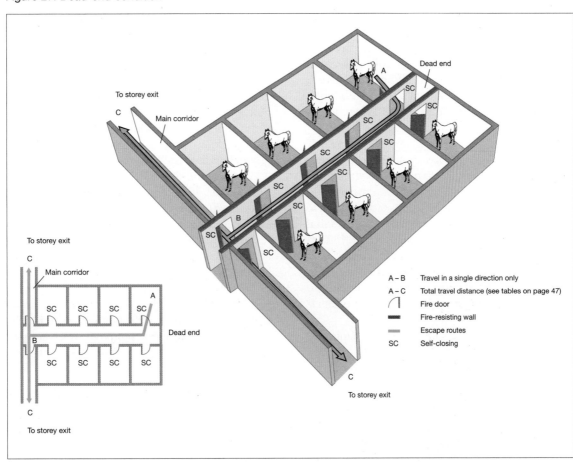

Figure 28: Dead-end condition provided with an alternative exit

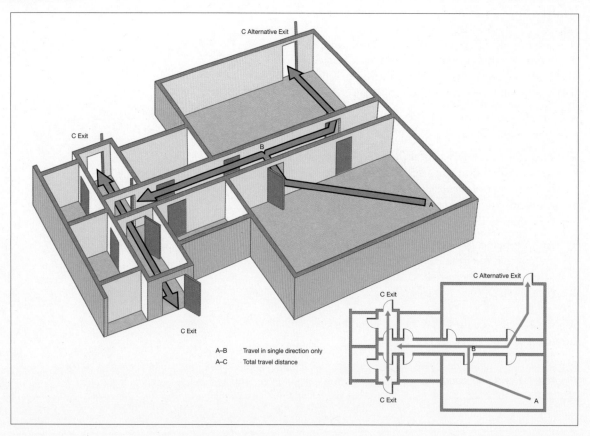

A–B   Travel in single direction only
A–C   Total travel distance

Figure 29: Dead-end condition with fire-resisting construction

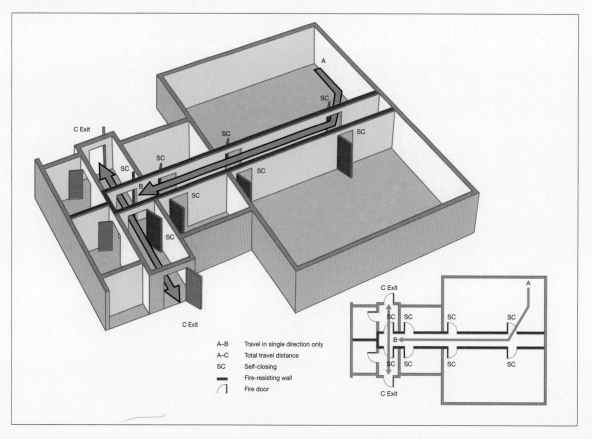

A–B   Travel in single direction only
A–C   Total travel distance
SC   Self-closing
▬   Fire-resisting wall
⌐   Fire door

Figure 30: Dead-end condition with automatic fire detection

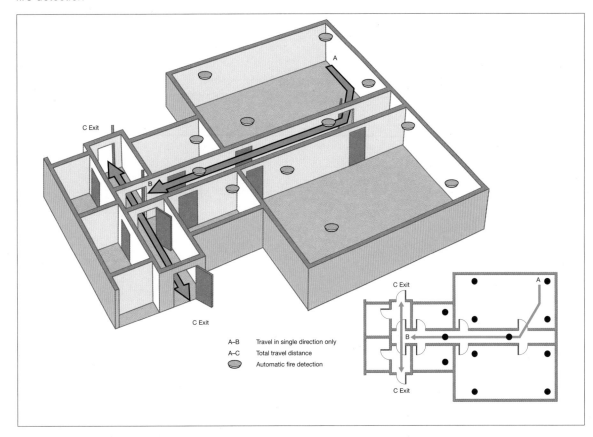

A–B   Travel in single direction only
A–C   Total travel distance
⬭   Automatic fire detection

Basement protection

In all animal buildings, other than those smaller premises detailed below, the stairways serving the upper floors should preferably not extend down to the basement. Wherever possible, all stairways to basements should be entered at ground level from the open air, and in such a position that smoke from any fire in the basement would not obstruct any exit serving the other floors of the building.

Where the stairway links a basement with the ground floor, the basement should be separated from the ground floor, preferably by two fire-resisting doors – one at basement level and one at ground floor level (see Figure 31).

As a minimum, any floor over a basement should achieve 60 minutes' fire resistance. Where this is impractical, and as long as no smoke can get through the floor, automatic smoke detection linked to a fire alarm system which is audible or visible throughout the premises could, as an alternative, be provided in the basement area. Where doubt exists, you should contact a competent person for more detailed advice.

Figure 31: Basement protection

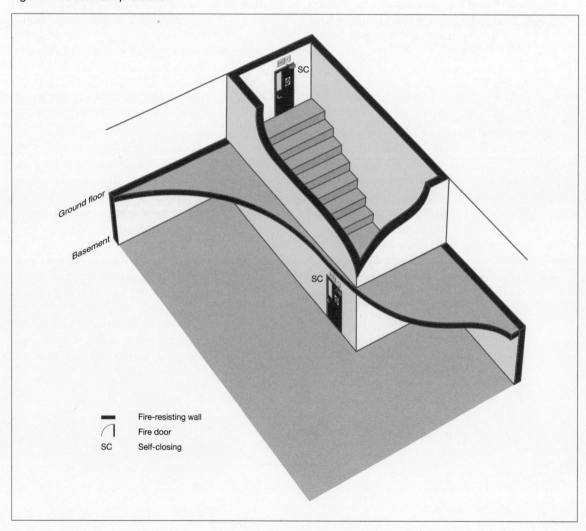

▬	Fire-resisting wall
⌐	Fire door
SC	Self-closing

Subdivision of corridors

If your animal or staff areas have corridors more than 30m in length, then generally these open floor areas and corridors should be subdivided with fire doors and, where necessary, fire-resisting construction to limit the spread of fire and smoke and to protect escape routes should a fire occur.

Where a corridor serves two storey exits, any subdivision should, wherever possible, ensure that no undivided length of corridor is common to more than one exit.

Cross-floor area partitions and doors that are provided solely for the purpose of restricting the travel of smoke to affect the entire floor area need not be fire doors and partitions, but will be considered suitable providing that they are of substantial construction and are capable of resisting the passage of smoke, and the doors are self-closing. Smoke should not be able to bypass these doors and partitions, e.g. above a false ceiling, or via alternative doors from a room, or adjoining rooms, opening on either side of the subdivision.

Generally, false ceilings should be provided with barriers or smoke stopping over any fire doors. Where the false ceiling forms part of the fire-resisting construction, this may not be necessary.

If you have doubts concerning subdivision of corridors, advice should be sought from a competent person.

Figure 32: Subdivision of corridor between two stairways or exits

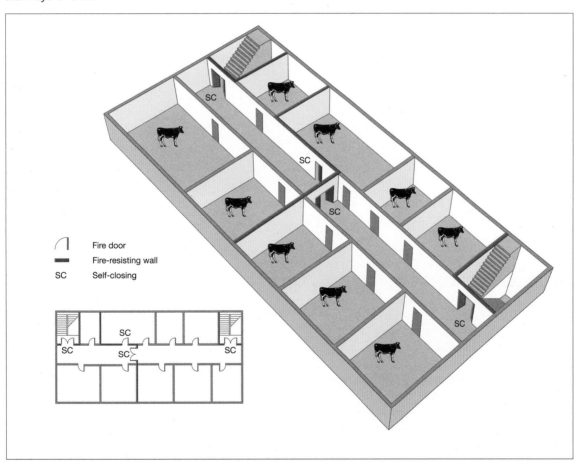

Stairway enclosures

In most two or more storey animal premises designed and built to modern building standards and served by more than one stairway, it is probable that at least one of the stairways will be protected by fire-resisting construction and will lead to a final exit. It is possible that you may have some stairways which have no fire protection to them: these are normally known as accommodation stairways.

If you have a fire protected stairway(s) then it is essential that you maintain that level of fire protection.

The benefit of protecting stairways from the effects of fire and smoke is that it allows you to measure your travel distance from the furthest point on the relevant floor level to the nearest storey exit rather than the final exit of the building.

If the buildings you occupy have floors which are occupied by different companies to your own, you will need to consider as part of your fire risk assessment the possibility that a fire may occur in another part of the building over which you may have no control, and which may affect the protected stairway(s) if allowed to develop unchecked.

If your fire risk assessment shows that this may be the case and people occupying the other floor levels would be unaware of a developing fire, it may require additional fire protection measures, e.g. an automatic fire detection and warning system.

You may find that the stairways in your buildings are provided with protected lobbies or corridors at each floor level (except the topmost floor). Although these provisions are not generally necessary for means of escape in multi-stairway buildings of less than 18m high, they may have been provided for other reasons. In all cases, protected corridors, lobbies and stairways must be maintained clear of combustibles and obstructions.

Figure 33: Examples of a stairway with protected lobby/corridor approach

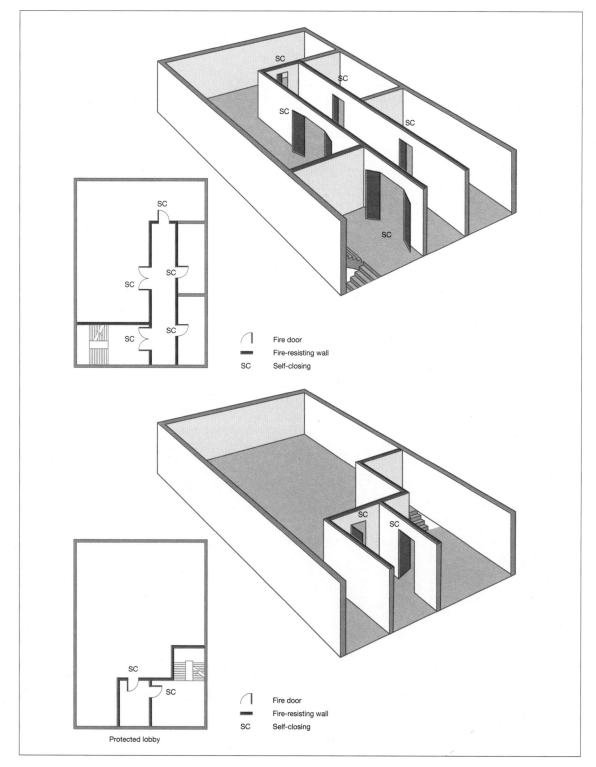

Fire door
Fire-resisting wall
SC   Self-closing

Protected lobby

Fire door
Fire-resisting wall
SC   Self-closing

Ideally, all stairway enclosures in your buildings should lead directly to an open-air final exit. If any of your stable buildings is provided with only one stairway from the upper floor(s) which does not lead directly to a final exit, one of the following arrangements should be adopted:

- the provision of a protected route from the foot of the stairway enclosure leading to a final exit; or

- two exits from the stairway should be provided, each giving access to a final exit via routes which are separated from each other by fire-resisting construction.

Figure 34: Examples of a protected route from a stairway to a final exit

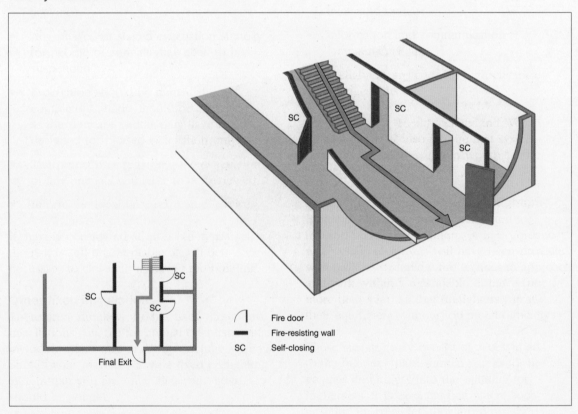

Separation of protected stairways

Where there are two or more protected stairways from the upper floor levels, the routes to the final exits should be separated by fire-resisting construction so that fire cannot affect more than one escape route at the same time.

Figure 35: Separation of protected stairways

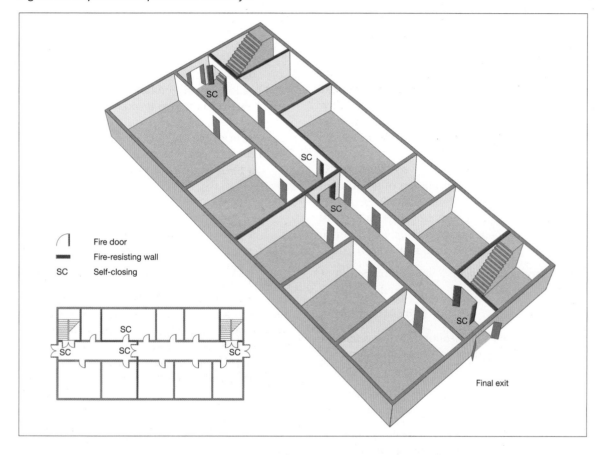

Creating a stairway bypass route

No one should have to pass through a protected stairway to reach another stairway. Options to avoid this include:

- using intercommunicating doors between rooms adjacent to the stairway;

- using balconies and other features to bypass the stairway; or

- provided there is sufficient space, creating a bypass corridor around the stairway enclosure.

Figure 36: A stairway bypass route

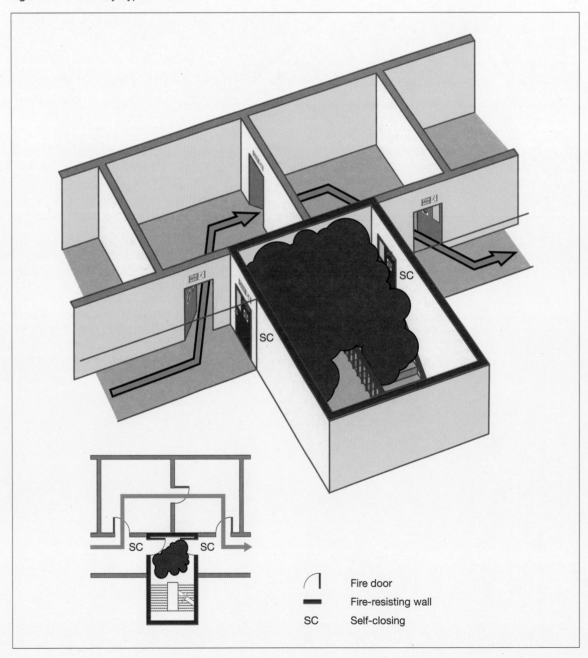

Fire door

Fire-resisting wall

SC   Self-closing

Width of stairs

In most circumstances, a stairway should be not less than 1m wide at any point along its route. In older style agricultural or equine buildings, stairways which are less than 1m wide may be considered, but only where a few people who are familiar with the stairway, e.g. stable staff, are likely to use it. Staircases less than 1m wide should not be used by members of the public, livery owners or other people unfamiliar with the building.

Reception offices and areas

Reception, office or enquiry areas should only be located at the base of stairways where the stairway is not the only one serving the upper floors, or the reception area is very small (less than 10m²) and with low fire risk contents.

Accommodation stairways

If you have stairways that are used for general communication and movement of all people at the stables, and they are not designated as fire escape stairs, then these stairs are termed accommodation stairways.

Consequently, they may not require fire protection and separation from the remainder of the floor levels, provided they do not pass through a fire compartment floor. (However, experience shows that many people will still continue to use these stairways as an escape route.)

Accommodation stairways should not form an integral part of the calculated fire escape routes; however, where your fire risk assessment indicates that it is safe to do so, then you may consider them for that purpose.

External stairways

To be considered a viable fire escape route, an external stairway must normally be protected from the effects of a fire along its full length. This means that all doors and windows (other than toilet windows) within 1.8m horizontally and 9m vertically should be to a fire-resisting standard. Windows should be in frames fixed shut, with doors effectively self-closing.

You should also consider protecting the external stairway from the effects of the weather, as the treads may become slippery, e.g. due to a build-up of algae, moss or ice. If this is not possible, you must ensure that the stairways are regularly maintained. Consider fixing non-slip material to the treads.

Figure 37: Protection to an external stairway

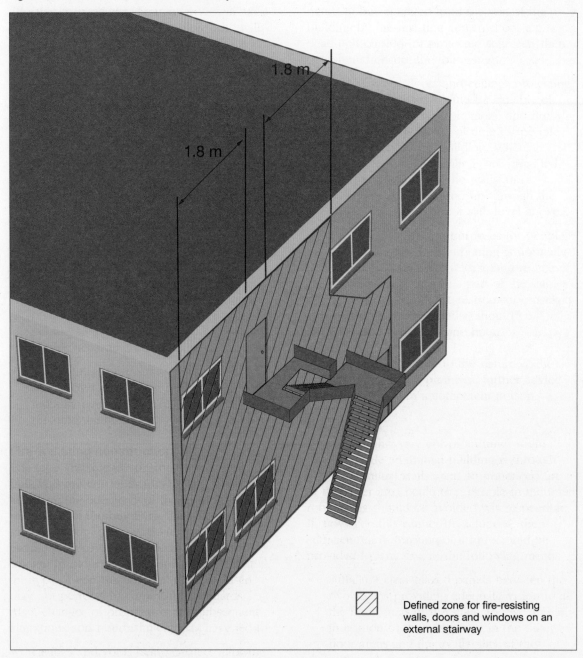

1.8 m

1.8 m

Defined zone for fire-resisting walls, doors and windows on an external stairway

Spiral and helical stairways

Existing spiral stairways that do not conform to BS 5395-2 are acceptable only in exceptional situations, e.g. for a maximum of 50 people (staff) and not for members of the public, visitors, etc. The stairway should not be more than 9m in height (ground to top floor level) and not less than 1.5m in diameter with adequate headroom. A handrail should be continuous throughout the full length of the stairway.

Helical stairways which do not conform to BS 5395-2 are not normally acceptable for escape by members of the public, visitors, livery owners, etc or for large numbers of people. They should be used as staff accommodation stairways only. However, they could be considered acceptable as an escape stairway for a limited number of able-bodied staff.

Roof exits

Only in very limited situations will it be reasonable for the fire escape route to cross a roof. Where this is the case, additional precautions will normally be necessary:

- The roof should be flat and the route across it should be adequately defined and well illuminated, where necessary, with normal electric and emergency lighting.

- The route should be non-slip and guarded with a protective barrier and handrail.

- The escape route across the roof and its supporting structure should be constructed as a fire-resisting floor.

- Where there are no alternatives other than to use a roof exit, any doors, windows, roof lights and ducting within 3m of the escape route should be to a fire-resisting standard.

- The exit from the roof should be in, or lead to, a place of reasonable safety where people can quickly move to a place of total safety.

Figure 38: An escape route across a roof

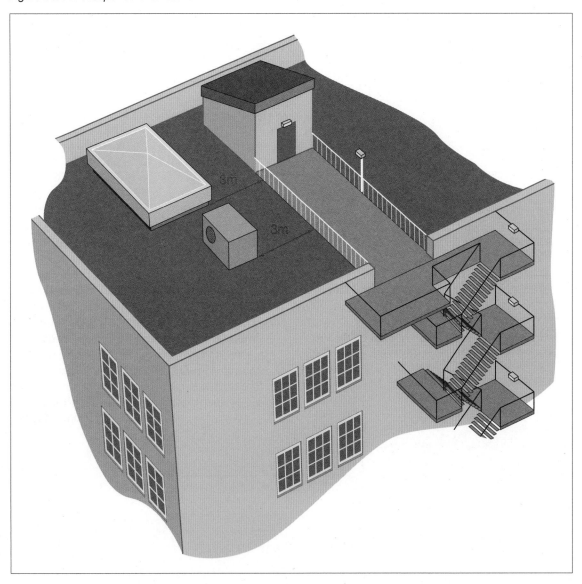

External escape routes should regularly receive routine inspections and maintenance to ensure they remain fit for use.

Revolving doors, wicket doors and roller shutters

Very few animal buildings will be fitted with revolving doors. If provided, they should not normally be considered as fire escape doors unless the leaves of the revolving doors can be quickly folded outwards by any person to form a clear opening upon pressure from within, or pass doors of the required exit width are provided next to the revolving door.

Ideally, smaller wicket doors or gates fitted to either up-and-over or sliding larger doors should have a minimum opening height of 1.5m. The bottom of the door should not be more than 250mm above the floor level, and the width of the wicket door should be preferably more than 500mm but not less than 450mm. Normally, wicket doors will only be suitable for up to 15 members of staff; however, in areas of a higher fire risk, e.g. combustible barns containing bedding and fodder storage, this should be reduced to a maximum of three people using this storage area at any one time.

Storage buildings, arenas, etc with loading and goods delivery doors, shutters (rolling, folding or sliding), up-and-over doors and similar openings are not normally suitable for use as a final exit. However, they may be suitable for escape from areas of normal and low risk provided they are not likely to be obstructed and can be easily and immediately opened manually. If normally power operated, on the failure of the power supplies these doors should be capable of being easily opened by a person inside or outside the building.

Final exit doors

Having good fire escape routes to a final exit will be of little benefit if the occupants are not able to get out of the buildings and quickly disperse away from the vicinity. It is also important to consider where people will go once they have evacuated the premises.

The matters that you should consider include the following:

- It is important that all final fire exit doors can be quickly and easily opened without the use of a key or security code in the event of a fire. Where possible, there should be only one fastening when the buildings are occupied.[2]

- The final escape exit door should not lead people into an enclosed yard or area from which there is no further escape.

- People evacuating from buildings or other structures should not cross the paths of animals being released from the stables.

Note: Your identified assembly points for people should not be in conflict with the safe and secure areas you have identified for assembling the animals following their release from the buildings.

Flexibility with regard to fire protection measures

A degree of flexibility will be required when applying this guidance, therefore the following principles have been provided to assist you in this task, as your range of animal premises may not exactly fit all or any of the examples illustrated.

The level of fire protection should be proportional to the risk of a fire occurring and the risk posed to the safety of all the occupants of the building, not forgetting the safety of the animals.

The higher the fire and life risk, the more intense the standards of fire protection will need to be. Therefore, your objective should be to reduce the fire risk to a level as low as reasonably practicable. Conversely, lower fire risks will need less intense levels of fire protection.

Where the risk cannot be reduced to a satisfactory level by fire prevention methods, then suitable protective measures should be put in place. Generally, the higher the fire risk, the shorter the fire escape travel distances required, to reduce the evacuation time accordingly.

[2] Further information on security fastenings can be found in Appendix C.

Some of the issues that may affect fire risk are identified at the beginning of this section under 'Evaluating, removing or reducing the risk and protecting from fire'. This list is not exhaustive as many of the factors are also covered in the earlier steps of the risk assessment process highlighted in Part 1. A safe, cost-effective solution to providing adequate means of escape from fire for the occupants will lower the risk to a level that is reasonable and practicable, by a combination of good fire prevention practices, sound fire protection measures and a robust approach to fire safety management.

Figure 39: Flexibility of fire protection measures

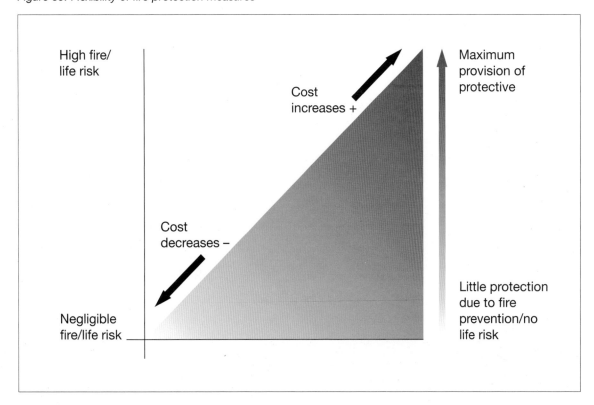

Flexibility in applying guidance – trading off or balancing fire protection measures

Your animal premises may not exactly fit the standards normally recommended in this guide and they may need to be applied in a flexible manner without compromising the life safety of all the occupants. Normally, a professional undertakes this; however, minor variations can normally be undertaken in a common-sense manner by most reasonable people.

For example, if the recommended travel distance is slightly in excess of the norm, e.g. 10% to 15%, it may be necessary to undertake any one, or a combination, of the following to compensate:

- provide earlier warning of fire in the form of suitable automatic smoke detection;

- revise the internal layout of the buildings to reduce travel distances;

- reduce the level of the fire risk by removing or reducing the quantity of combustible materials and/or ignition sources;

- reduce the numbers of people, i.e. non-employees;

- reduce the numbers of other people permitted into any of the buildings at any one time;

- limit areas to trained staff only (no public or livery owners); or

- increase staff training and education.

Note: The above list is not exhaustive and is only used to illustrate some examples of 'trade-offs' to provide equally safe premises.

Your animal premises may have already been provided with a number of active fire protection measures, e.g. a comprehensive automatic fire detection system, smoke control systems and life safety water fog or fire sprinkler systems, to provide for greater flexibility in the use of the premises, as opposed to the normal passive fire protection measures. Therefore you should always check the existing provisions first, and if necessary seek advice from a competent person if:

- you need to substantially move away from this guidance;

- your premises are high risk; or

- your stables or other premises are more than 11m high.

4.2 Typical equine building examples

The following examples demonstrate generally acceptable layouts, showing appropriate fire protection measures to ensure the safety of all people using your premises. These are not intended to be prescriptive or exhaustive but merely to assist you in understanding how the principles of means of escape may be applied in practice.

In all animal buildings where there is accommodation, residential or otherwise, located directly over stables and other animal accommodation, all the staircases and floors should be protected and sealed with fire-resisting materials, because of the potential for a rapid generation of smoke from a fire in highly combustible bedding and forage materials.

Note: You only need to consider those diagrams which most closely resemble your premises.

Table 3: Typical building examples

Ground floor animal premises with a single exit (may include a mezzanine)	See Figure 40
Ground floor animal premises with more than one exit	See Figure 41
Two-storey animal premises with a single stairway	See Figure 42
Two-storey animal premises, including basement, with a single stairway	See Figure 43
Three-storey animal premises, including basement, with a single stairway	See Figure 44
Larger three-storey animal premises, including basement, with a single stairway	See Figure 45
Animal premises, ground and up to three upper storeys, with a single stairway	See Figure 46
Large animal premises with more than one stairway	See Figure 47

Note: If any of your buildings exceeds the above parameters, your should seek expert advice.

Single-storey animal buildings

Ground floor animal premises with a single exit (may include a mezzanine)
If your fire risk assessment shows that people using the mezzanine floor level would be unaware of a fire, it may require you to provide additional fire protection measures, e.g. an automatic fire detection and warning system.

A mezzanine covering more than half of the floor area may need to be treated as a separate floor (see two-storey buildings).

Figure 40: Ground floor premises with a single exit (including a mezzanine)

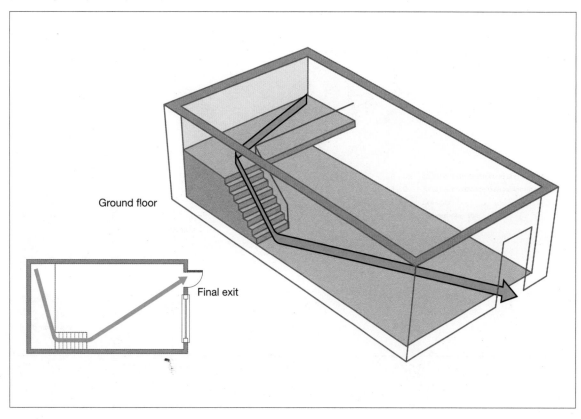

Ground floor

Final exit

Ground floor animal premises with more than one exit

In all animal accommodation premises, it is preferable to provide alternative fire escape routes. All sets of exit doors should be of a suitable width for releasing and exiting the animals.

Figure 41: Ground floor premises with more than one exit

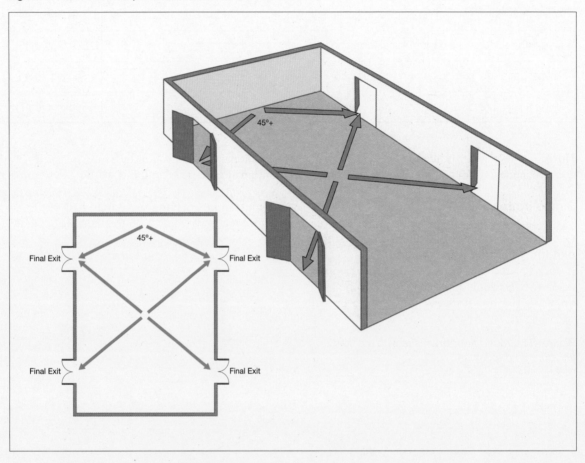

Multi-storey animal buildings

In the majority of multi-storey stables and other premises, two or more stairways will need to be provided for escape purposes. Premises that are provided with only a single stairway from upper floors or basement or lower level storeys may require special consideration as this will be the only escape route available to people from these floors.

Stairways, if unprotected from fire, can rapidly become affected by heat and smoke, cutting off the escape route and allowing fire spread to other floors. However, if adequately protected, fire escape stairways can be regarded as places of reasonable safety to enable all people to escape to a place of total safety.

Figure 42: Two-storey premises: lower risk premises

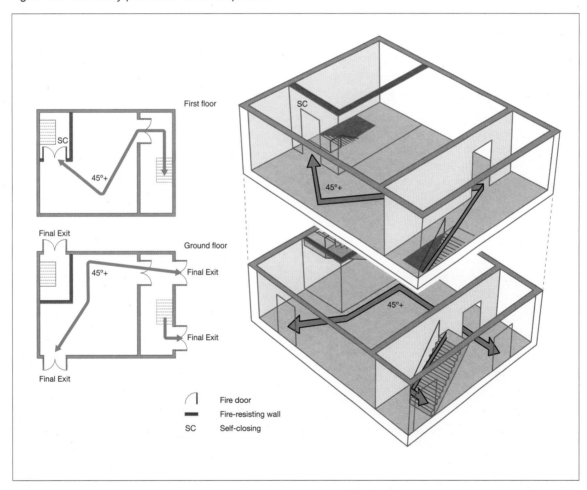

Fire door
Fire-resisting wall
SC   Self-closing

In animal premises with a basement or lower floor level and a simple layout, an open stairway is acceptable providing the following apply:

- Travel from the furthest point on either floor to the final exit is within the overall suggested travel distance (see Table 2).

- The final exit should be visible and accessible from the discharge point of the stairway at ground floor level.

- The area near the exit is maintained clear of all combustibles and obstructions.

If your fire risk assessment shows that people using either floor would be unaware of a fire, it may require additional fire protection measures, e.g. an automatic fire detection and warning system.

Three-storey animal premises, including basement, with a single stairway

In animal premises with a basement or lower floor level, ground and first floor served by individual stairways, the layout shown below will be generally acceptable providing that the following apply:

- The furthest point in the basement or lower floor level to the exit door to the stairway is within the overall suggested travel distance (see Table 2).

- The furthest point on the other floors to the final exit is within the overall suggested travel distance (see Table 2).

- The stairway from the basement to the ground floor level is enclosed by fire-resisting construction and leads to an open-air final exit.

- The area near the exit is maintained clear of combustibles and obstructions.

- The final exit should be visible and accessible from the discharge point of the stairway at ground floor level.

- High fire risk rooms should generally not open directly into a fire-resisting stairway.

If your fire risk assessment shows that people using any floor would be unaware of a fire, it may require additional fire protection measures, e.g. an automatic fire detection and warning system.

If you do not have this stairway configuration, and depending on the outcome of your fire risk assessment, it may be that an equivalent level of safety can be achieved by other means.

Figure 43: Three-storey premises, basement, ground and one upper floor

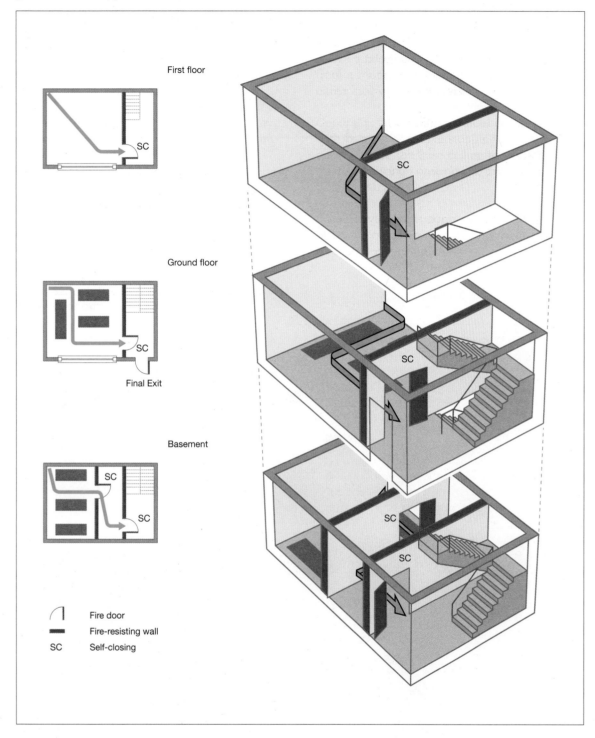

First floor

SC

Ground floor

SC

Final Exit

Basement

SC

SC

SC

SC

SC

Fire door

Fire-resisting wall

SC   Self-closing

Animal premises, ground and up to three upper storeys, with a single stairway

In animal premises with a ground floor and up to three upper storeys served by a single stairway, it is important to understand that you are unlikely to be able to meet the suggested travel distance to a final exit (see Table 2). In these circumstances it is necessary for the stairway to be suitably protected by a fire-resisting enclosure as shown. If the stable buildings you occupy have floors which are occupied by different companies or organisations to your own, you will need to consider, as part of your own fire risk assessment, the possibility that a fire may occur in another part of the building over which you may have no control, and which may affect the existing protected stairway if allowed to develop unchecked.

The layout shown below will be generally acceptable providing that the following apply:

- The furthest point on all of your floors to the storey exit is within the overall suggested travel distance (see Table 2).

- The escape route should lead to a final exit.

- The fire-resisting stairway must at all times be maintained clear of combustibles and obstructions.

- Where the building incorporates a basement, a fire-resisting lobby or corridor between that basement and the protected stairway should separate any stairway from the basement.

- High fire risk rooms should generally not open directly into a fire-resisting stairway.

If your fire risk assessment shows that people occupying any of the other floors would be unaware of a developing fire, it may require additional fire protection measures, e.g. an automatic fire detection and warning system.

If you do not have this stairway configuration, and depending on the outcome of your fire risk assessment, it may be that an equivalent level of safety can be achieved by other means.

Where your building has more than three upper storeys and a single staircase, you should seek advice from a competent person.

Figure 44: Four-storey premises, ground and up to three upper floors

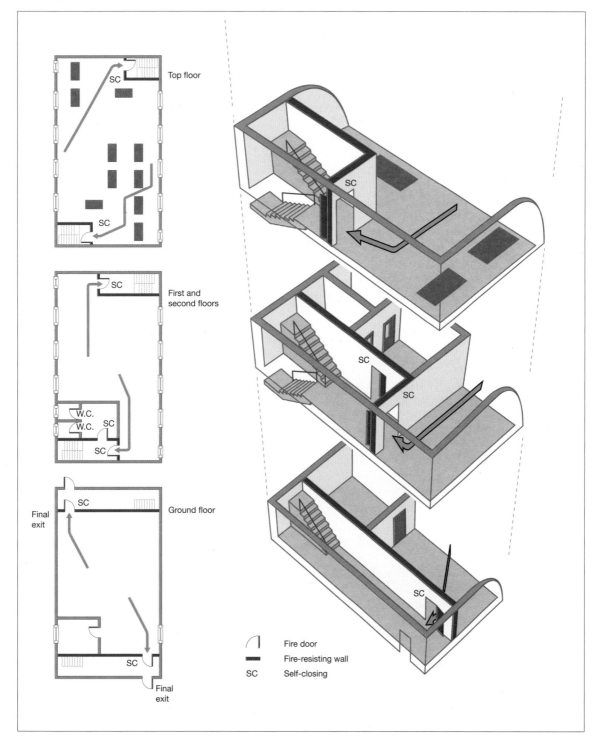

Top floor

SC

SC

First and second floors

SC

W.C.

W.C.

SC

SC

SC

SC

Final exit

Ground floor

SC

SC

SC

SC

Final exit

⌐ Fire door

▬ Fire-resisting wall

SC Self-closing

Large animal premises with more than one stairway

In most modern animal premises designed and built to modern building standards and served by more than one stairway, it is probable that at least one of the stairways will be protected by fire-resisting construction and will lead to a final exit. It is also possible that you may have some stairways which have no fire protection to them; these are normally known as accommodation stairways.

If you have a fire protected stairway(s) then it is essential that you maintain that level of fire protection. In the case of accommodation stairways, it is not normal to consider them for means of escape purposes; however, where your fire risk assessment indicates that it is safe to do so, then you may consider them for that purpose.

The benefit of protecting stairways from the effects of fire and smoke is that it allows you to measure your travel distance from the furthest point on the relevant floor level to the nearest storey exit rather than the final exit.

If the buildings you occupy have floors which are occupied by different companies to your own, you need to consider as part of your fire risk assessment the possibility that a fire may occur in another part of the building over which you may have no control, and which may affect the protected stairway(s) if allowed to develop unchecked.

You may find that all the stairways in your building are provided with protected lobbies. Although these lobbies are not generally necessary for means of escape in multi-stairway buildings of less than 18m high, they may have been provided for other reasons.

In taller buildings (in general those over five storeys, excluding basements), the person who has overall control of common areas of the building may need to seek advice from a competent person.

The layout shown below illustrates these principles. You also need to consider the following:

- Stairways must always be maintained clear of combustibles and obstructions.

- Where the building incorporates a basement or lower ground floor level, a fire-resisting lobby or corridor between that basement and the protected stairway should separate any stairway from the basement.

- If your fire risk assessment shows that people using any floor would be unaware of a fire, it may require additional fire protection measures, e.g. an automatic fire detection and warning system.

If you do not have a protected stairway, and depending on the outcome of your fire risk assessment, it may be that an equivalent level of safety can be achieved by other means; however, it is strongly recommended that you seek advice from a competent person.

The figure below illustrates a multi-storey building fitted with a firefighting shaft, which is required for specific types of buildings. However, this guide is not intended to deal with buildings of this size. If the premises you occupy is situated in a building like this, you should seek the guidance of a competent person.

It is unlikely that there will be many standard animal premises with these layouts, unless they are located in larger buildings, e.g. a race course.

Figure 45: Tall building with a firefighting shaft

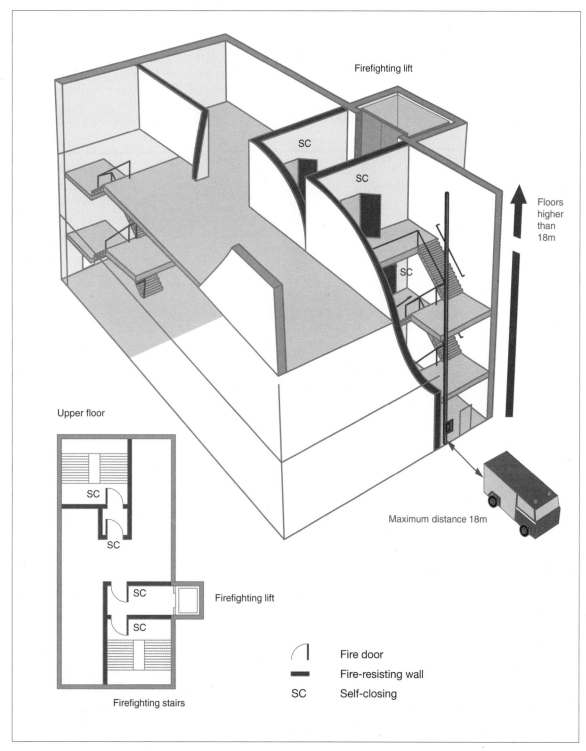

Firefighting lift

SC

SC

SC

Floors higher than 18m

Upper floor

SC

SC

SC

SC

Firefighting lift

Firefighting stairs

Maximum distance 18m

⌐ Fire door

▬ Fire-resisting wall

SC Self-closing

Provision of gates or openings in the arena perimeter barrier(s)

Where a perimeter barrier is in place and the arena is used as part of the escape route, it should be fitted with gates or openings allowing egress in an emergency from the area of activity.

If a viewing area is divided by structural means, each division should have sufficient gates or openings to evacuate all the spectators in that division. When open, no door or gate should obstruct any gangway, passage or stairway.

Further guidance on gates and openings is available in the Guide to Safety at Sports Grounds.[3]

Seating and gangways

The type of seating arrangements adopted will vary with the use to which the event or venue is put. Venues should only be used for closelyseated audiences if your risk assessment shows that it is safe to do so.

Where your event or venue is licensed, there may be additional conditions in the licence concerning how seating may be set out.

Audiences seated in rows will first have to make their way to the end of the row before being able to use the escape routes provided. Seating and gangways in an assembly space should therefore be so arranged as to allow free and ready access direct to the exits.

In fixed seats, there should be a clear space of at least 305mm between the back of one seat and the front of the seat behind it (or the nearest point of the seat behind it, for automatic tip-up seats, see Figure 46). Gangways should be adequate for the number of seats served and at least 1.05m wide. There should be no projections that diminish these widths.

In general, no seat should be more than seven seats away from a gangway. If temporary seating is provided, it should be secured in lengths of not fewer than four seats (and not more than 12). Each length should be fixed to the floor.

Standing and sitting in gangways, or in front of any exit, should not be permitted.

If booster seats are provided for small children that will prevent seats returning to an upright position, you need to consider the implications on means of escape.

For sports grounds, you should consult the Guide to Safety at Sports Grounds.[4] Detailed information of seating layout is given in BS 5588-6.[5]

Figure 46: Clear space between seating

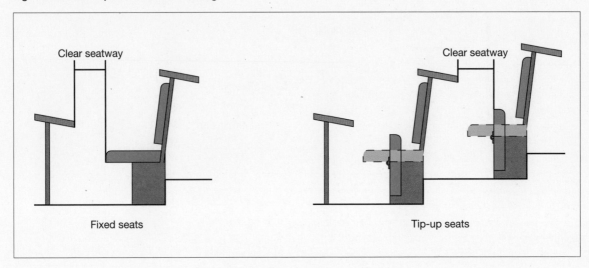

Fixed seats | Tip-up seats

Clear seatway

[3] Guide to Safety at Sports Grounds. Department of National Heritage/The Scottish Office Fourth Edition 1997. ISBN 0 11 300095 2.
[4] Ibid
[5] BS 5588 Part 6: *Fire precautions in the design construction and use of buildings. Code of practice for places of assembly.* British Standards Institution.

Section 5 Further guidance on emergency escape lighting

In all cases where your stables or animal establishment are used during the hours of darkness, it will be necessary to provide sufficient primary illumination for general safe movement and in particular to illuminate all the escape routes and exits. In some exceptional cases, ambient light from adjacent areas, e.g. street lighting, might be sufficient, but in most cases a separate source of electrically powered lighting will be necessary. Where mains power is not available, power will need to be provided from another source, e.g. a central generator or individual powered lighting units.

There are two forms of lighting that you should consider:

- escape lighting – natural or artificial escape lighting normally used within all your premises, which may be needed to allow people to escape safely; and

- emergency lighting – lighting that will function if the normal lighting fails. In most cases this type of emergency lighting must light automatically.

The primary purpose of the emergency lighting is to illuminate all the escape routes, but a supplementary role is the illumination of fire exit signage and other safety equipment.

The size and type of your premises or stables and the risk to the occupants will determine the complexity and extent of the emergency lighting required. Borrowed lighting may be suitable in very small premises where the light is from a dependable source, e.g. street lamps, and it will adequately illuminate escape routes. These options may not be available for those stable buildings located in more rural or less populated areas.

Where borrowed lighting is not suitable then a number of rechargeable torches, located in strategic positions, can be considered.

Single 'stand-alone' emergency lighting units may be sufficient in small premises and these can sometimes be combined with exit or directional signs. The signage positioned on the lighting units should not significantly reduce the level of general illumination.

For larger or extensive buildings, a more comprehensive system of fixed automatic emergency lighting is likely to be needed, particularly in those buildings with extensive or complex floor areas, basements or where there is a significant number of staff or members of the public. Alternatively, mains or generator-powered floodlights, with a suitable back-up power supply, may be acceptable.

You will have identified the escape routes when carrying out your fire risk assessment and need to ensure that they are all adequately illuminated. If there are escape routes that are not permanently illuminated, such as external stairs, then a switch, clearly marked 'Escape lighting', or some other means of switching on the lighting should be provided at the entry to that area/stairs.

An emergency lighting system provided for escape purposes would normally cover the following:

- each fire exit door;

- fire escape routes;

- fastenings and catches to open the fire exit doors;

- intersections of corridors;

- outside each final exit and on external fire escape routes;

- emergency fire escape signs;

- staircases, so that each flight receives an adequate level of illumination;

- changes in floor level;

- windowless rooms and toilet accommodation exceeding 8m²;

- firefighting equipment;

- fire alarm call points;

- equipment that would need to be shut down in an emergency;

- lifts; and

- floor areas, including the inside of stables, stores areas, equine shops, the staff's welfare accommodation and open-plan floor areas, which are greater than 60m².

Note: The level or proposed level of emergency lighting will need to be increased in buildings occupied by animals if staff and firefighters will be expected to access the building to try and release the animals from their stalls or the building.

As a high percentage of stables and animal establishments are located in areas of the country that are devoid of any normal street lighting, the external yard areas should also be provided with emergency lighting to assist people exiting the buildings and yard areas and for the removal of animals to a safe enclosure.

Emergency lighting can be both 'maintained', i.e. on all the time, or 'non-maintained', which only operates when the normal lighting fails. Units are available with durations of between one and three hours. In practice, the three-hour units are the most popular and can help with maintaining limited continued use of your premises during a power failure (other than in an emergency situation). Maintained lighting is used particularly in buildings that accommodate large numbers of people, e.g. arenas with seated and/or standing audiences.

Figure 47: Luminaires

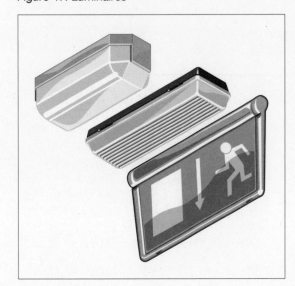

Emergency lighting can be stand-alone dedicated units or incorporated into normal light fittings. There are highly decorative versions of these for those areas that demand aesthetically pleasing fixtures. Power supplies can be rechargeable batteries integral to each unit, a central battery bank or an automatic generator.

To complement emergency lighting, people, especially those unfamiliar with the premises, can be assisted in identifying exit routes by the use of way-finding equipment. Way-finding systems usually comprise photo-luminescent material or miniature incandescent strips, forming a continuous marked escape route at lower level. These systems have proved particularly effective when people have had to escape through smoke, including for partially sighted people. They may be useful in certain stable buildings where they can provide marked routes on floors, and in multi-storey buildings they can direct people to escape routes which are seldom used.

If you decide that you need to install emergency lighting or modify your existing system, a competent person should carry out any work in accordance with the appropriate standards.

To maintain the effectiveness of all the emergency lighting units located in stables and other dusty or dirty environments, management procedures will need to ensure that the lighting units are kept clean and clear of all airborne sediment, cobwebs and dust.

Figure 48: A 'way-guidance' system

Maintenance and testing of emergency lighting

All emergency lighting systems should be regularly tested and properly maintained to an appropriate standard. Most existing systems will need to be manually tested. However, some modern systems have self-testing facilities that reduce routine checks to a minimum.

Depending on your type of installation, you should be able to carry out most of the routine tests yourself. The method of test will vary. If you are unsure about how to undertake these tests, you should contact your supplier or other competent person.

Figure 49: A test key

Test facilities often take the form of a 'fishtail' key inserted in a special switch, either near the main fuse board or adjacent to relevant light switches.

Typically, testing would include:

- a daily visual check;

- a monthly function test for a maximum of one quarter of the rated duration; and

- an annual full discharge test (for units over three years old).

Particular care needs to be taken following a full discharge test as batteries typically take up to 24 hours to recharge, and the premises should not be reoccupied until the emergency lighting system is fully functioning. The appropriate standards are BS 5266 and BS EN 1838.

Section 6 Further guidance on signs and notices

Escape signs

In small and simple animal premises, a single sign indicating the alternative exit(s) might be all that is needed. In larger and more complex premises, a series of signs directing people along the escape routes towards the final exit might be needed.

A fire risk assessment, other than in very small animal premises and stables, that determines that no escape signs are required as trained staff will always be available to assist visitors, members of the public or other people to escape routes, is unlikely to be considered acceptable to an enforcing authority.

Many people with impaired or poor vision retain some sight and are able to recognise changing or contrasting colour to provide them with visual clues when moving around a building or structure. Columns that are painted a different colour to the walls and highlighted changes in level may be sufficient.

For people with impaired vision, a well-managed 'buddy system', continuous handrails or a sound localisation system may be appropriate.

Positioning of escape route signs

The presence of other signs (such as advertising and customer information) or shop dressing in equine retail shops can distract attention from, or obscure the visibility of, escape signs. This could affect people's ability to see and understand escape signs, particularly in the event of a fire evacuation. Great care should therefore be taken to ensure that all fire escape signs are not overwhelmed by displays or advertising.

Escape signs should meet the following criteria:

- Exit signs should provide clear, unambiguous instruction with sufficient information to enable people to safely leave a building in an emergency.

- Every fire escape route sign should, where necessary, incorporate or be accompanied by a directional arrow. Arrows should not be used on their own.

- If the escape route to the nearest exit is not obvious, then sign(s) should indicate it.

- Signs should be positioned so that a person escaping will always have the next escape route sign in sight.

- Exit signage to the nearest fire exit door should be clearly visible from any part of the floor area.

- Escape route and exit signs should not be fixed to doors, as they will not be visible if the door is open.

- Signs mounted above doors should be at a height of between 2.0m and 2.5m above the floor. Signs on walls and hanging signs should be mounted between 1.7m and 2.0m above the floor.

- All exit signage that is likely to be affected by dust or cobwebs should be the subject of regular cleaning to ensure the signs are clearly visible.

Figure 50: Euro sign

Figure 51: BS-type sign

---

[6] The Royal National Institute of the Blind estimates that only about 4% of visually impaired people are totally blind.

Note: Either type of sign (BS or Euro) will be acceptable but different types should not be mixed.

Escape sign design

The legibility of fire escape signs is determined by the size of the sign, its level of illumination and the distance over which it is viewed. The signs used within the same premises should follow a consistent design pattern or scheme. You should not rely on a few outsized signs, which may encourage people to travel to a particular escape route when other, more appropriate routes should be used.

In multi-occupied animal premises, co-operation between all the respective responsible people, including, if necessary, the managing agent or landlord, should be sought to ensure that, as far as possible, all signs in the building conform to a single pattern or scheme.

Other safety signs and notices

A number of other mandatory signs, such as the blue and white 'Fire door – keep shut' signs on fire doors and 'Fire action' notices, may also be necessary.

Figure 52: Fire door 'keep shut' notice

Signs should also indicate non-automatic fire safety equipment if there is any doubt about its location, e.g. fire extinguishers that are kept in cabinets or in recesses.

Hazard warning signage relating to compressed gas cylinders, chemicals and cleaning materials, veterinary medicines and any indoor deep water therapeutic treatment areas will need to be displayed on the outside of all buildings.

Staff notices

In small stables and yards where there is a limited number of people present at any one time, it may be reasonable to provide staff with verbal reminders of the actions to be taken in the event of a fire. You could consider providing this in a short written statement that can be delivered with staff pay slips every six months.

In multi-occupied, larger and more complex animal premises or where there is a high turnover of staff, a more considered approach for staff notices and instructions will be necessary.

In addition to positioning the fire instructions notice on escape routes adjacent to fire alarm call points, position additional copies of fire instructions where staff frequently assemble in the stables, e.g. the tack room, office, canteen, locker rooms, etc.

Figure 53: Fire action notice

If your premises are routinely expected to accommodate large numbers of people whose first language is not English, you may need to consider providing instructions in more than one language. The interpretation should always convey an identical message.

Section (4) of the Riding Establishments Act 1964 provides that a local authority, in deciding whether to grant a licence for a riding establishment must have regards to (among other things) the need to secure that appropriate steps will be taken for the protection and extrication of horses in the case of fire and [...] instructions as to action to be taken in the event of fire, with particular regard to the extrication of horses, will be kept displayed in a prominent position on the outside of the premises'. The instructions should preferably not be displayed in a high fire risk or combustible building.

The fire instructions notice will also include:

- the name, address and telephone number of the licence holder or some other responsible person;

- the extrication procedures and arrangements for the release of the horses;

- fire routine and procedures;

- means for giving warning in the event of fire;

- no smoking notices;

- the provision of firefighting equipment; and

- the means of exit in an emergency.

Illumination

All signs and notices will require illumination to ensure they are conspicuous and legible. There are a number of options available to achieve this, such as:

- external illumination;

- internal illumination;

- photoluminescence; and

- self-luminescence.

Further advice on the above may be sought from a suitable signage supplier or other competent person.

Appropriate standards

Guidance on compliance with health and safety legislation governing signs has been published by the HSE.

Detailed guidance on the legibility, design and use of safety signs can be found in BS 5499-5:2002.

Section 7 Further guidance on recording, planning, informing, instructing and training

7.1 The management of fire safety

Fire safety records

Keeping up-to-date records of your fire risk assessment can help you effectively manage the fire strategy for your site and demonstrate how you are complying with fire safety law.

Even if you do not have to record the fire risk assessment, it can be helpful to keep a record of any co-operation and exchange of information made between employers and other responsible people for future reference.

At complex sites, it is best to keep a dedicated record of all maintenance of fire protection equipment and training. There is no single 'correct' format specified for this. Suitable record books are available from trade associations and may also be available from your local enforcing authority.

In all cases the quality of records may also be regarded as a good indicator of the overall quality of the fire safety management structure. Fire safety records could include:

- a record of the sites use, means of escape, fire fighting equipment, fire alarms, and high risk areas;

- details of any significant findings from the fire risk assessment and any action taken;

- testing and checking of escape routes, including final exit locking mechanisms, such as panic bars, push pads and any electromagnetic devices;

- testing of fire-warning systems, including weekly alarm tests and periodic maintenance by a competent person;

- recording of false alarms;

- testing and maintenance of emergency escape lighting systems;

- testing and maintenance of fire extinguishers, hose reels and fire blankets etc.;

- if appropriate, testing and maintenance of other fire safety equipment such as fire suppression systems;

- training of relevant people and fire evacuation drills;

- planning, organising, policy and implementation, monitoring, audit and review;

- maintenance and audit of any systems that are provided to help the fire and rescue service; and

- the arrangements in a multi-occupied sites for a co-ordinated emergency plan or overall control of the actions you or your staff should take if there is a fire.

Other issues that you may wish to record include:

- the competence, qualifications and status of the persons responsible for carrying out inspections and tests;

- the results of periodic safety audits, reviews, inspections and tests, and any remedial action taken;

- all incidents and circumstances which had the potential to cause accidents and monitor subsequent remedial actions; and

- a record of the building or structure use, the fire prevention and protection measures in place and high-risk areas.

The range and type of records necessary will become more detailed as the site and its use becomes more complex and so the level of competence of the person carrying out the assessment will need to be higher.

Your documentation should be available for inspection by representatives of the enforcing authority.

A blank version of this form is available at www.communities.gov.uk/fire.

The 'safe person' concept can be applied to the management of fire safety in a similar way to the culture of health, safety and welfare in the workplace. Good management of fire safety in your animal premises will help you to ensure that any fire safety matters that arise are always addressed effectively. In small stables and livery yards, the manager or owner maintaining and planning fire safety in conjunction with general health and safety can achieve this.

Larger animal premises and livery yards

In larger animal organisations it is good practice for a principal person or manager to have overall responsibility for fire safety. It may be appropriate for this person to be the manager designated with overall responsibility for health and safety.

An animal organisation's fire safety policy (like its health and safety policy) should be sufficiently flexible to allow modification. This is particularly important when managers or responsible people have to work daily with other businesses in the same building. It should be recognised that fire safety operates at all levels within an organisation and therefore local managers should be able to develop, where necessary, a local action plan for their premises.

The animal premises' policy should be set out in writing and may cover such things as:

- who will hold the responsibility for fire safety at board level;

- who will be the responsible person for each stable or yard (this will be the person who has overall control, usually the manager);

- the arrangement whereby managers will, where necessary, nominate in writing specific people to undertake particular tasks in the event of a fire; and

- the arrangement whereby regional or area managers of large multi-building locations should monitor and check that individual managers are meeting the requirements of the fire safety law.

You should have a plan of action to bring together all the features that you have evaluated and noted from your fire risk assessment so that you can logically plan what needs to be done. It should not be confused with the emergency plan, which is a statement of what you will do in the event of a fire.

The plan of action should include the actions you intend to take to reduce the hazards and risks that you have identified and to implement the necessary protection measures.

You will need to prioritise these actions to ensure that any findings that identify people (and animals) in immediate danger are dealt with straight away, e.g. unlocking fire exits. In other cases where people or animals are not in immediate danger but action is still necessary, it may be acceptable to plan this over a period of time.

7.2 Fire safety records

Keeping up-to-date records of your fire risk assessments can help you effectively manage the fire strategy for your premises and demonstrate how you are complying with fire safety law.

In larger and more complicated animal premises, it is best to keep a dedicated record of all maintenance of fire protection equipment and training. There is no one 'correct' format specified for this. Suitable record books are available from trade associations and may also be available from your local enforcing authority.

Fire safety records could include:

- details of any significant findings from the fire risk assessment and any action taken;

- testing and checking of escape routes, including final exit locking mechanisms, such as panic bars, push pads and any electromagnetic devices;

- checking the animal release arrangements from their stalls or enclosures;

- testing of fire warning systems, including weekly alarm tests and periodic maintenance by a competent person;

- recording of false alarms;

- testing and maintenance of emergency lighting systems;

- testing and maintenance of all the provided firefighting equipment and arrangements;

- if appropriate, testing and maintenance of other fire suppression systems;

- training of relevant people and fire evacuation drills;

- planning, organising, policy and implementation, monitoring, audit and review;

- maintenance and audit of any systems that are provided for the assistance of the fire service; and

- any arrangements in large, multi-occupied yards and stables for a co-ordinated emergency plan or overall control of the actions you or your staff should take in the event of a fire.

The range and type of records necessary will become more detailed as the animal premises and their use become more complex; accordingly, the person carrying out the assessment will need to have an appropriate level of competence.

Figure 54 below is an example of how you could record this information as you move through Steps 1 to 4.

Figure 54: Recording information

Step 1
Identify fire hazards

Step 2
Identify people and animals at risk from fire

Step 3
Evaluate hazards and risks from fire
Evaluate people and animals at risk from fire
Remove or reduce risks and hazards
Remove or reduce risks to people
Fire safety measures provided to protect from residual risk

Step 4
Item included in emergency plan?
Written instructions and information passed to:
Name:
Type:
Responsibility:
Who you have co-operated and co-ordinated with
Training received:
Name:
Date:

Figure 55 below is an example of recording some individual stages of the process in more detail. In this example, the form is also used as a tool to assess the risk of a fire starting. You will note in Step 3, the evaluation stage, the assessor is asked to make a separate judgement for risk and hazard and describe the level of risk as high, normal or low.

Figure 55

Step 1	Step 3.1 Evaluate risk and hazard		Step 3.3		Step 3.5 to 3.10
Sources of ignition and fuel	Risk – of ignition	Hazard – if a fire starts	Remove the risk	Reduce the risk	Fire safety measures provided to protect against residual risk
Heating lamps in stables	Normal	High – fire will spread to fodder and bedding	Unable to remove	Ensure a clear distance of 2m between lamps and the fodder/bedding	Staff trained to use 9 litres water fire extinguishers in the stables if safe to do so
Deep-fat fryer in kitchen/canteen – risk of ignition	High	Fire spread to kitchen ceiling and adjacent cupboards	Unable to remove	Remove cooking facility – substitute with a microwave	Escape routes to final exit are within the suggested distance. Provide a fire blanket, and suitable firefighting equipment and staff training.
Step 2	Step 3.2		Step 3.4		Step 3.5 to 3.10
Identify people at risk	Evaluate risks to people		Remove the risk	Reduce the risk	Fire safety measures provided to protect from residual risk to people
No natural light in the feed store	High– staff unable to find exit door when working late if power fails		Unable to remove risk	Unable to reduce risk	Provide emergency lighting on escape route.
Disabled people permitted in stables	Low – access available for disabled people in the stables only		N/A	Staff will be present in the stables at all times and will assist disabled people to leave.	Travel distance to all final exit doors satisfactory

In animal premises with 'engineered fire safety strategies', a fire policy manual should be provided in addition to any other records.

Enforcing authorities would expect a fire engineering policy manual to conform to the structure set out in BS 7974-0 Section 5: Reporting and presentation.

Fire safety audit

A fire safety audit can be used alongside your fire risk assessment to identify what fire safety provisions exist in your premises.

When carrying out a review of your fire safety risk assessment, a pre-planned audit can quickly identify if there have been any significant changes which may affect the fire safety systems and highlight whether a further full fire risk assessment is necessary.

Appendix A has a sample checklist that can be used to help construct an audit process for your organisation. This is only a sample of the most common features of a fire safety management programme and should be adapted to suit your own particular needs.

7.3 Emergency plans

Your emergency should be appropriate to your event or venue. It should be kept on site and available for inspection and could include:

- how people will be warned if there is a fire;

- where people should assemble after they have left the premises and procedures for checking whether the premises have been evacuated;

- identification of key escape routes, how people can gain access to them and escape from them to a place of total safety;

- how the evacuation to a place of safety should be carried out;

- assessing the adequacy of the number of staff to supervise the evacuation;

- what training staff require and the arrangements for ensuring that this training is given;

- how the fire and rescue service, and any other necessary services, will be called and who will be responsible for doing this;

- arrangements for fighting the fire;

- information on post incident plans;

- the action to be taken by staff in the event of fire, including those who have specific fire safety functions (e.g. nominated deputies, fire marshals, etc.);

- the arrangements for any people at particular risk, for example, contractors, maintenance workers, members of the public, people with a disability;

- any specific arrangements for parts with high fire risk;

- evacuation procedures for everyone on the site, including details of escape routes;

- arrangements for calling the fire and rescue service and informing them of any special hazards.

You should include a sketch showing, where relevant:

- essential features such as the layout of the site, escape routes (including those from any structures such as a park ride or exhibit);

- the number, type and location of fire-fighting equipment available, for example extinguishers, hose reels, fire blankets;

- the location of:

  - manually-operated fire alarm call points and control equipment for the fire alarm;

  - any automatic fire-fighting system and control valve;

  - the main electrical supply point, the main water shut-off valve and (where appropriate) the main gas or oil shut-off valves; and

  - any special hazards or highly flammable substances.

For larger venues and events it is likely that the local authority and emergency services will prepare their own plan for response to a major incident at the event or venue. In these cases you will need to co-ordinate your plan with the local authority response plan so they are compatible – for example making sure that your arrangements for evacuation will not prevent the emergency services from gaining entry to the site by blocking the access route.

After the emergency plan has been prepared, prominent notices should be displayed on site giving clear instructions about what to do in case of fire. They should describe how to raise the alarm and give the location of the assembly points to which people escaping from the site should report.

On small sites, the plan can take the form of a simple fire action notice which should be posted where staff can read it and become familiar with it.

In multi-occupancy, larger and more complex events or venues, the emergency plan will need to be more detailed. It should be compiled only after consultation with other occupiers and other responsible people, e.g. owners who have control over different events within the site. In most cases this will require that an emergency plan covering the whole site/event/venue will be necessary. It will help if you can agree on one person to co-ordinate this task.

When planning an event you should consult the local fire and rescue service and consider the following issues:

- safe access in and out of the site for fire and rescue service vehicles;

- means of calling the emergency services;

- the availability of main services (particularly water for fire fighting);

- the slope or unevenness of the ground;

- impact of adverse weather conditions (such as heavy rain); and

- the availability of car parking (so that it can be properly arranged to avoid obstructing emergency access).

Your emergency plan should not be a stand alone schedule of actions to be undertaken in the event of an emergency. It should form part of your contingency planning arrangements for the variety of occurrences that may require the responsible person's attention and action during your event, which may include post fire actions. Examples of such occurrences include:

- lost children;

- animals on the loose;

- responding to crowd behaviour due to alcohol consumption;

- people with a disability;

- inclement weather;

- first aid;

- failure of sanitary arrangements;

- power failure;

- people with personal belongings (especially valuables) still in the site;

- people in a state of undress (e.g. stage performers);

- people wishing to rejoin friends; and

- getting people away from the event or venue (e.g. to transport);

Children

The particular needs of children should be considered. Parts of site used solely by children (e.g. play grounds) or where children are present require special precautions. Children should be supervised at all times. If a child care facility is provided, consideration needs to be taken of the behaviour of the parents in a fire situation, e.g. the parents first action will be locate and ensure the safety of their children. Therefore, evacuation planning should consider the parents needs to ensure the safety of the child.

Animals

People with pets, and those who have the responsibility for animal care, at venues such as a zoo, circus, and equestrian events, will have additional burdens. Special needs and legal responsibilities they may have should be accommodated prior to the open air event, so that in the event of a fire, they are clear as to the course of action they should take to ensure not only their safety, but, so far as possible, that of the animals within their care.

You should develop an action plan that considers the welfare of the animals. The necessary means for safe evacuation and the provision of holding areas, appropriate to the size and number of animals to be handled must be clearly identified. Consideration should also be given to the physical impacts and dangers of animals on the escape of the occupants. Bedding materials are a considerable fire risk. Any potential ignition sources such as heating or lighting should be controlled and the location/storage of such materials must be assessed to ensure that adequate animal and people safety is achieved. You should organise this in advance.

7.4 Information, instruction, co-operation and co-ordination

Supplying information

You must provide easily understandable information about the existing fire safety measures in place to ensure a safe escape from the building and how they will operate, for example:

- any significant risks to staff and others that have been identified in your fire risk assessment or any similar assessment carried out by another user and responsible person at the animal premises;

- the fire prevention and fire protection measures and procedures at your stables, and where they impact on staff, visitors and others who may be at the animal premises;

- the procedures for raising the fire alarm and provisions for fighting a fire at the animal premises; and

7 See HSE guidance HSG 65

- identifying those people who have been nominated with specific responsibilities and duties at the animal premises.

Even if you do not legally have to record the fire risk assessment, it would be helpful to keep a record of any co-operation and exchange of information made between occupiers and other responsible people for future reference.

The responsible person will need to ensure that all staff and, where necessary, others who work at the stables receive written information in a way that can be easily understood. This might include any special instructions to particular people who have been allocated a specific task, such as the release of the animals from their stalls, shutting down mechanical equipment or the sweeping system to guide members of the public, visitors, etc to the nearest exits and assembly points.

Duties of stable staff and employees to give information

Staff and employees also have a duty to take reasonable care for the safety of themselves and other people who may be affected by their activities. This includes the need for them to inform their employer or the occupier of the stables of any activity that they consider would present a serious and immediate danger to their own safety and that of others.

Dangerous substances

The HSE publishes guidance[7] on specific substances where appropriate information may need to be provided. If any of these, or any other substance that is not included but nevertheless presents more than a slight risk, is present at your animal premises, then you must provide such information to staff and others, specifically you must:

- name the substance and the risks associated with it, e.g. how to use it safely or store the product to avoid creating highly flammable vapours or explosive atmospheres;

- identify any legislative provisions that may be associated with the substance;

- allow employees access to the hazardous substances safety data sheet; and

- where necessary, supply information to the emergency services where there are significant hazards, e.g. veterinary medication and treatment.

Information to the emergency services

In the case of dangerous substances, where the assessment identifies a risk greater than 'a slight risk' and it is not possible to sufficiently reduce it further, then the responsible person must communicate their findings to the emergency services to enable them to prepare their own response procedures.

It will also be helpful to provide information to the emergency services in instances that do not involve dangerous substances, e.g. the temporary loss of a firefighting facility.

Instruction

You will need to carefully consider the type of instructions to the staff and other people working and visiting your animal premises. Written instructions must be concise, comprehensible and relevant and therefore must be reviewed and updated as new working practices and hazardous substances are introduced. This is also relevant to any increase in the number of animals being stabled.

Inclusive access and employment policies mean that people with special mobility needs or learning difficulties may now be present in a range of animal premises. Your fire risk assessment should also consider whether further instruction or guidance is necessary to ensure that your evacuation strategy is appropriate and understood by everyone at the animal premises.

Instructions will need to be given to people delegated to carry out particular tasks, for example:

- removing additional security, bolts, bars or chains on final exit doors before the start of business to ensure that escape routes are accessible;

- daily, weekly, quarterly and yearly checks on the range of fire safety measures (in larger equine premises);

- safety considerations when closing down the premises at the end of the day, e.g. removing rubbish, ensuring sufficient exits are available for people who remain and closing fire doors and shutters;

- leaving hazardous substances in a safe condition when evacuating the stable buildings;

- the safe storage of hazardous substances at the end of the working day;

- ensuring that everyone in large equestrian organisations with many buildings within the yard and cartilage and any special security zones know how to use internal emergency telephones to raise the alarm;

- the procedures and actions for ensuring the safety of those animals still confined within buildings;

- specific responsibilities that must be carried out on hearing the fire alarm;

- how staff will assist members of the public/ visitors to leave all the animal buildings;

- 'sweeping' of the public areas by staff, to guide people to the nearest exit;

- deciding which emergency animal enclosure should be used to hold the evacuated animals;

- designating particular areas of the indoor animal manège, indoor arenas, vets room, etc for supervisors to check that no person or animal remains;

- calling the emergency services;

- carrying out the evacuation roll calls;

- taking charge at the assembly area(s);

- meeting and directing fire engines, providing information on water supplies, special hazards and risks, etc; and

- cover arrangements when the nominated people are on leave.

Co-operation and co-ordination

Where you share animal premises with others (this includes people who are livery owners or in partnership), each responsible person, i.e. each employer, owner or other person who has control over any part of the premises, will need to co-operate and co-ordinate the findings of their separate fire risk assessments to ensure the fire precautions and protection measures are effective throughout all the stable buildings. This could include such matters as:

- co-ordinating an emergency plan;[8]

- identifying the nature of any special risks and how they may affect others in or about the animal premises;

- the presence of people with impairments or special mobility needs;

- the presence of any residential accommodation that may be affected by a fire in any of the animal buildings;

- identifying any specific fire prevention and protection measures;

- identifying any measures to mitigate the effects of a fire; and

- arranging contacts with the local external emergency services.

7.5 Fire safety training

Staff training

The actions of all the animal premises staff in the event of fire breaking out in any of the animal buildings are likely to be crucial to their safety and that of other people who may be in any of the animal buildings, and to the safety of the animals. All staff should receive basic fire safety induction training within the first few days of working at the premises and attend refresher sessions at pre-determined intervals.

You should ensure that all your staff, including volunteers and contractors, are told about the animal premises' emergency plan and procedures and are shown all the fire escape routes.

The training should take account of the findings of the fire risk assessment, be easily understood by all those attending and consider the role that those members of staff will be expected to carry out if a fire occurs.

This may vary in large animal premises, with some staff being appointed as fire marshals/ wardens or given some other particular role for which additional training will be required.

In addition to the guidance given in Part 1, Step 4, as a minimum all staff should receive information, instruction and training on:

- the items listed in your emergency plan;

- the importance of fire doors and other basic fire prevention measures;[9]

- where relevant, the appropriate and safe use of the animal premises' firefighting equipment;

- the importance of reporting to the assembly area(s);

- exit routes and the operation of exit devices, including physically walking these routes; and

- general matters such as permitted smoking areas, restrictions on cooking, and the farrier's hot shoeing other than in designated areas.

Staff training is necessary:

- when new staff (including volunteers) commence employment or are transferred into the premises;

- when changes have been made to the emergency plan and the preventive and protective measures;

- where working practices and processes or people's responsibilities change;

- to take account of any changed fire risks to the safety of staff, volunteers and visitors; and

- to ensure that all staff know what they have to do to safeguard themselves, the animals and all people at the stables.

---

[8] See Step 4.2 for features of an emergency plan.
[9] See Step 4.2 for further details on emergency plans.

Training should be repeated as often as is considered necessary and take place during working hours.

Whatever training you decide is necessary to support your fire safety strategy and emergency plan, it should be verifiable and supported by management.

Enforcing authorities may look to examine your fire logbook/records as evidence that adequate training has been given.

Fire marshals/wardens

Staff nominated to undertake the role of fire marshals (often called fire wardens) will require more comprehensive training. Their role may include assisting members of the public or visitors from all parts of the premises, checking designated areas to ensure everyone has left, using firefighting equipment if safe to do so, liaison with the fire service on arrival, shutting down vital or dangerous equipment, releasing the animals and performing a supervisory/managing role in any fire situation.

Training for this role may include:

- detailed knowledge of the fire safety strategy for the premises;

- basic understanding of human behaviour in smoke and fires;

- basic understanding of animal behaviour in smoke and fires (including those identified as being kickers or otherwise dangerous);

- how to encourage people to use the most appropriate escape route;

- how to search safely and recognise situations and areas that are considered unsafe to enter;

- the difficulties that some people, particularly if disabled, may have in escaping and any special evacuation arrangements that have been pre-planned;

- additional training in the use of firefighting equipment;

- an understanding of the purpose of any fixed firefighting equipment such as sprinklers or water fog/spray systems; and

- reporting of faults, incidents and near misses that could have started a fire.

Fire drills

Once the emergency plan has been developed, and suitable training given, you will need to evaluate its effectiveness. The best way to do this is to perform a fire drill. This should be carried out at least annually, or as determined by your fire risk assessment, and you will need to consider staff turnover.

A well-planned and executed fire drill will confirm an understanding of the training and provide helpful information for future training.

At least one of the fire drills during the year should include releasing the animals and taking them to one of the emergency enclosures.

The responsible person should determine possible objectives of the drill such as:

- to identify any weaknesses in the evacuation strategy;

- to identify any weakness in the procedures for the release of the animals;

- to test the procedures following any recent alteration or changes to working practices, including an increase in the number of animals;

- to familiarise new members of staff with procedures; and

- to test the arrangements for evacuating disabled people.

Who should take part?

Within each animal building, the evacuation should be for all the occupants except those who may need to ensure the security of the premises, or people who, on a risk-assessed basis, are required to remain with particular equipment, processes that cannot be closed down or animals that cannot be left unattended.

Animal premises that consist of several sizable buildings on the same site should be dealt with one building at a time over an appropriate period, unless the emergency procedure dictates otherwise.

Carrying out the fire drill

For all animal buildings that have more than one fire escape route, the emergency escape plan should be designed to evacuate all people and animals on the assumption that one of the widest fire exit doors or stairways is unavailable due to the presence of smoke or fire.

It is advisable not to mix animals with people when designing the escape routes.

A designated person located at a suitable point on an exit route could simulate this. Applying this scenario to different escape routes during each fire drill will encourage individuals to use alternative escape routes, which they may not normally use.

When carrying out the fire drill you might find it helpful to:

- circulate details concerning the fire drill and inform/remind all people of their duty to participate. It may not be beneficial to have 'surprise drills' as the health and safety risks introduced, including to the animals' safety, may outweigh the benefits;

- ensure that all equipment and/or machinery can be safely left;

- nominate observers;

- inform the receiving company if your fire warning system is monitored. If the fire and rescue service is normally called directly from your premises, ensure that this does not happen. It should be part of the fire drill to ensure that those people nominated to call the fire service are familiar with the procedures;

- inform all members of the public, visitors, contractors, etc, if they are present. It is not unreasonable for the public, visitors or contractors to take part in the fire drill process; and

- ask a member of staff at random to set off the fire warning facility by operating the nearest alarm point. This will indicate the level of knowledge regarding the location of the nearest fire warning point.

At least once a year your fire drill should include the release and evacuation of all the animals, including taking them to the emergency holding areas.

Where you invite your local fire and rescue service to participate in the evacuation of the animals to their identified holding area, they may not be aware of the problems of mixing stallions with mares.

The roll call

Carry out a roll call as soon as possible at the designated assembly point(s), and note any people (and animals) who are unaccounted for.

In a real evacuation this information will need to be passed to the fire and rescue service on arrival.

You may need to consider an assembly point at one of the animal enclosures, with a roll call for those people nominated to release the animals.

Once the roll call is complete, allow people to return to their duties and buildings. If the fire warning system is monitored, inform the receiving station that the drill has now been completed and record the outcomes of the drill in your fire logbook.

Note: Accounting for all the animals should only be carried out once all people have been accounted for.

Monitoring and debrief

Throughout the duration of the fire drill, the responsible person and nominated observers should pay particular attention to:

- communication difficulties with regard to the roll call and establishing that everyone is accounted for;

- the use of nearest available fire escape routes as opposed to common circulation routes;

- difficulties with the opening of final exit doors;

- difficulties experienced by people with disabilities;

- difficulties experienced with the evacuation of the animals;

- roles of specified people, e.g. fire wardens;

- inappropriate actions, e.g. stopping to collect personal items, etc; and

- windows and doors not being closed as people leave.

On-the-spot debriefs are useful to discuss the fire drill, encouraging feedback from everybody. Later, reports from fire wardens/marshals and observations from people should be collated and reviewed. Any conclusions and remedial actions should be recorded and implemented.

Section 8 Quality assurance of fire protection equipment and installations

Fire protection products and related services should be fit for their purpose and properly installed and maintained in accordance with the manufacturer's instructions or a relevant standard.

Third-party certification schemes for fire protection products and related services are an effective means of providing the fullest possible assurances, offering a level of quality, reliability and safety that non-certificated products may lack. This does not mean goods and services that are not third-party approved are less reliable, but there is no obvious way in which this can be demonstrated.

Third-party quality assurance can offer comfort, both as a means of satisfying you that the goods and services you have purchased are fit for purpose, and as a means of demonstrating that you have complied with the law.

However, to ensure the level of assurance offered by third party schemes, you should always check whether the company you employ sub-contracts work to others. If they do, you will want to check that the subcontractors are subject to the level of checks of quality and competence as the company you are employing.

Your local fire and rescue service, fire trade associations or your own trade association may be able to provide further details about third party quality assurance schemes and the various organisations that administer them.

Appendix A

Example fire safety maintenance checklist

As a starting point in formulating your animal premises' fire safety policy, this sample fire safety checklist can be used for small animal premises that do not have complex fire safety measures. It should not be used as a substitute for carrying out a full fire risk assessment.

You will need to incorporate into this sample the recommendations of manufacturers and installers of the fire safety equipment/systems that you may have installed in your premises.

Any ticks in the grey boxes should result in further investigation and appropriate action as necessary. In larger and more complex premises you may need to seek the assistance of a competent person to carry out some of the checks.

	Yes	No	N/A	Comments
General				
Is there an identified testing/maintenance system for all the equipment?	☐	☐	☐	
Is there a recording system for all training, drills, etc?	☐	☐	☐	
Daily checks (not normally recorded)				
Fire escape routes				
Can all fire exits be opened immediately and easily?	☐	☐	☐	
Are all internal and external escape routes clear?	☐	☐	☐	
Fire warning arrangements				
Do you have systems for warning all people in the event of fire?	☐	☐	☐	
Are hand gongs/air horns in place?	☐	☐	☐	
Is the mains electrical fire alarm panel indicator showing 'normal' (usually a green light)?	☐	☐	☐	
Have there been any recent false alarms?	☐	☐	☐	
Do the stables use a public address system to warn staff and visitors of fire?	☐	☐	☐	
Escape lighting				
Is there any obvious damage to luminaires?	☐	☐	☐	
Are all the luminaires clear from dust or dirt?	☐	☐	☐	
Firefighting equipment				
Is all firefighting equipment in place?	☐	☐	☐	
Is all the fire equipment clearly visible?	☐	☐	☐	
Weekly checks				
Escape routes				
Do all emergency fastening devices to fire exits (push bars and pads, etc) work correctly?	☐	☐	☐	
Are external routes clear and safe?	☐	☐	☐	

	Yes	No	N/A	Comments

Weekly checks *continued*

Fire warning systems

	Yes	No	N/A	Comments
Does the testing of a manual call point send a signal to the indicator panel? (Take the system off-line if applicable.)	☐	☐	☐	
Did the alarm system work correctly?	☐	☐	☐	
Did staff and other people hear or see the fire alarm?	☐	☐	☐	
Did any linked fire protection systems (e.g. smoke curtains, ventilation systems) operate correctly?	☐	☐	☐	
Do all visual and/or vibrating alarms work?	☐	☐	☐	
Do voice alarm systems work correctly? Was the message understood?	☐	☐	☐	

Escape lighting

	Yes	No	N/A	Comments
Are charging indicators (if fitted) visible?	☐	☐	☐	
Does the emergency generator start correctly?	☐	☐	☐	

Firefighting equipment

	Yes	No	N/A	Comments
Is there any obvious damage?	☐	☐	☐	
Additional items from manufacturer's recommendations.	☐	☐	☐	

Monthly checks

General

	Yes	No	N/A	Comments
Have all emergency generators been tested? (Normally run for one hour.)	☐	☐	☐	

Escape routes

	Yes	No	N/A	Comments
Do all electronic release mechanisms on escape doors work correctly? Do they 'fail safe' in the open position?	☐	☐	☐	
Do all automatic opening doors on escape routes 'fail safe' in the open position?	☐	☐	☐	
Do all roller shutters provided for fire compartmentation work correctly?	☐	☐	☐	
Are external escape stairs safe to use?	☐	☐	☐	
Do all internal self-closing fire doors work correctly?	☐	☐	☐	

Escape lighting

	Yes	No	N/A	Comments
Do all luminaires operate on test for a maximum of one quarter of their rated value?	☐	☐	☐	

Firefighting equipment

	Yes	No	N/A	Comments
Is the pressure in 'stored pressure' fire extinguishers correct?	☐	☐	☐	
Additional items from manufacturer's recommendations.	☐	☐	☐	

Three-monthly checks

General

	Yes	No	N/A	Comments
Are the emergency water supply tanks, ponds, etc at their normal capacity level?	☐	☐	☐	
Are vehicles blocking fire hydrants or access to buildings?	☐	☐	☐	
Has any smoke control/ventilation system been tested?	☐	☐	☐	
Additional items from manufacturer's recommendations.	☐	☐	☐	

	Yes	No	N/A	Comments
Six-monthly checks				
General				
Has staff training been carried out?	☐	☐	☐	
Has a fire evacuation drill been carried out?	☐	☐	☐	
Has a fire evacuation drill been carried out involving the animals?	☐	☐	☐	
Has any firefighting or emergency evacuation lift been tested by a competent person?	☐	☐	☐	
Has any installed fire suppression system been tested by a competent person?	☐	☐	☐	
Have the release and closing mechanisms of any fire-resisting compartment doors and shutters been tested by a competent person?	☐	☐	☐	
Fire warning system				
Has the system been checked by a competent person?	☐	☐	☐	
Escape lighting				
Do all luminaires operate on test for one third of their rated value?	☐	☐	☐	
Additional items from manufacturer's recommendations.	☐	☐	☐	
Annual checks				
General				
Has staff training been carried out?	☐	☐	☐	
Escape routes				
Do all fire-resisting self-closing doors fit correctly?	☐	☐	☐	
Escape lighting				
Do all luminaires operate on test for their full rated duration?	☐	☐	☐	
Has the system been thoroughly checked by a competent person?	☐	☐	☐	
Firefighting equipment				
Has all the firefighting equipment been checked by a competent person?	☐	☐	☐	
Miscellaneous				
Has the dry/wet rising fire main (if installed) been tested?	☐	☐	☐	
Have external access roads and hard standing for the fire service been checked?	☐	☐	☐	
Have firefighters' switches for electrical equipment been tested?	☐	☐	☐	
Has the fire hydrant bypass flow valve control been tested?	☐	☐	☐	
Are fire engine directional signs in place?	☐	☐	☐	

Appendix B

Example of significant findings

Risk Assessment – Record of significant findings[1]		
Risk assessment for	**Assessment undertaken by**	
Venue/event	Date	
Location	Completed by	
	Signature	
Sheet number	**Floor/area**	**Use**

Step 1 – Identify fire hazards		
Sources of ignition	**Sources of fuel**	**Sources of oxygen**

Step 2 – People at risk

Step 3 – Evaluate, remove, reduce and protect from risk[2]

(3.1) Evaluate the risk of the fire occuring

(3.2) Evaluate the risk to people from a fire starting in the premises

(3.3) Remove and reduce the hazards that may cause a fire

(3.4) Remove and reduce the risks to people from a fire

Assessment review		
Assessment review date	**Completed by**	**Signature**

Review outcome (where substantial changes have occurred a new record sheet should be used)

Notes:

(1) The risk assessment record of significant findings should refer to other plans, records or other documents as necessary.

(2) The information in this record should assist you to develop an emergency plan; coordinate measures with other 'responsible persons' at the event or venue; and to inform and train staff and inform other relevant persons.

Appendix C

Fire-resisting separation, fire doors and door fastenings

Fire-resisting separation

General

The building materials from which your stables and animal premises are constructed may determine the speed with which a fire may spread, affecting the escape routes that people and animals will use. A fire starting in a building constructed mainly from readily combustible material will spread faster than one in a building where modern fire-resisting construction materials have been used. Where non-combustible materials are used and the internal partitions are made from fire-resisting materials, the fire will be contained for a longer period, allowing more time for the occupants to escape.

As a result of building regulations requirements, you will probably already have some walls and floors that are fire-resisting and limitations on the surface finishes to certain walls and ceilings.

You will need to consider whether the standard of fire resistance and surface finishing in the escape routes is satisfactory, has been affected by wear and tear or alterations and whether any improvements are necessary.

The following paragraphs give basic information on how fire-resisting construction can provide up to 30 minutes protection to escape routes and protection for those people releasing animals from their stalls.

This is the standard recommendation for most situations. Having read these paragraphs, if you are unsure of the level of fire resistance necessary, you should consult a fire safety expert.

Fire-resisting construction

The fire resistance of a wall or floor is dependent on the quality of construction and materials used.

Animal buildings containing large quantities of readily combustible fodder and bedding materials, which produce considerable heat and large quantities of smoke when they burn, will need special consideration as to the most suitable materials to use and the quality of workmanship for protecting fire escape routes and ceilings/floors above the animal premises and to divide up large open animal premises floor areas into fire compartments.

It is unlikely that the standard of fire resistance to protect fire escape routes and ceilings/floors above them from fire and collapse will exceed 30 minutes. For open-floor buildings accommodating numerous animal stalls, dividing the floor areas up into fire compartments from the floor to the underside of the ceiling or roof should be to a standard of at least one hour, especially where quantities of readily combustible fodder and bedding are kept.

Common examples of types of construction that provide 30-minute fire resistance to escape routes and prevent fire and smoke spread, if constructed to the above standards are:

- internal framed construction wall, non-load bearing, consisting of 72mm x 37mm timber studs at 600mm centres and faced with 12.5mm of plasterboard with all joints taped and filled;

- internal framed construction, non-load bearing, consisting of 25swg (or thinner) channel section steel studs at 600mm centres faced with 12.5mm of plasterboard with all joints taped and filled; and

- masonry cavity wall consisting of solid bricks of clay, brick earth, shale, concrete or calcium silicate, with a minimum thickness of 90mm on each leaf.

Figure 56: Fire-resisting construction

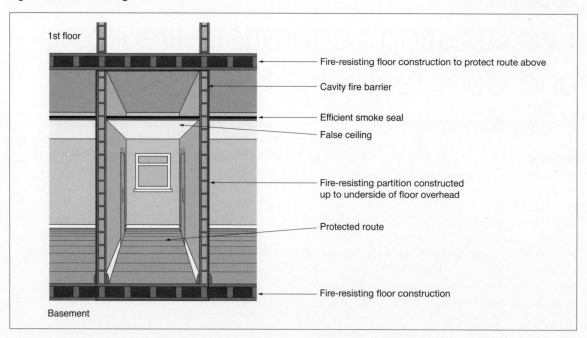

1st floor — Fire-resisting floor construction to protect route above

Cavity fire barrier

Efficient smoke seal
False ceiling

Fire-resisting partition constructed up to underside of floor overhead

Protected route

Fire-resisting floor construction

Basement

There are other methods and products available which will achieve the required standard of fire resistance and may be more appropriate for the existing construction in your animal premises, tack room, blanket store, etc. If there is any doubt as to the nature of the construction present, then further advice should be sought from a competent person.

Fire-resisting floors

The fire resistance of floors will depend on the existing floor construction as well as the type of ceiling finish beneath. If you need to upgrade the fire resistance of your floor it may not be desirable to apply additional fire resistance to the underside of an existing ceiling.

In older buildings, there may be a requirement to provide fire resistance between beams and joists.

A typical example of a 30-minute fire-resisting timber floor is tongue and groove softwood of not less than 15mm finished thickness on 37mm timber joists, with a ceiling below of one layer of plasterboard to a thickness of 12.5mm with joints taped and filled and backed by supporting timber.

There are other, equally valid, methods and products available for upgrading floors. If you are in any doubt you should seek the advice of a competent person and ensure that the product is installed in accordance with instructions from the manufacturer or supplier.

Fire-resisting glazing

The most common type of fire-resisting glazing is 6mm Georgian wired glazing, which is easily identifiable. Clear fire-resisting glazing is available and can quickly be identified by a mark etched into the glass, usually in the corner of the glazed panel, to confirm its fire-resisting standard. The glazing should have been installed in accordance with the manufacturer's instructions, or the appropriate standard, to ensure that its fire-resisting properties are maintained.

The performance of glazed systems in terms of fire resistance and external fire exposure should, wherever possible, be confirmed by test evidence. Alternatively, where there is a lack of test information, an assessment of the proposed construction should be sought from suitably qualified people.

Fire separation of voids

A common problem encountered with fire separation is fire-resisting partitions which do not extend above false ceilings to the underside of the roof or the true ceiling height. This may result in unseen fire spread and a loss of vital protection to the escape routes. It is important therefore as part of your fire risk assessment to carefully check that all such partitions have been installed correctly.

Compartmentation

In buildings which contain large quantities of highly combustible materials, i.e. hay, straw, etc, a small fire will very quickly spread to involve the entire contents of the building.

Only the very quickest of actions by staff, using water from a nearby fire hose, will have any chance of controlling the rapid development and spread of the fire.

To prevent total involvement of the entire stock, storage buildings should be divided up into fire compartments from floor level up to the underside of the roof. The compartment walls should be constructed of fire-resisting materials to not less than a four-hour fire-resisting standard.

CLASP and SCOLA type construction

CLASP (Consortium of Local Authorities Special Programme) and SCOLA (Second Consortium of Local Authorities) are systematic methods of construction that were developed to provide consistent building quality, while reducing the need for traditional skilled labour. They consist of a metal frame upon which structural panels are fixed. This results in hidden voids through which fire may spread. It is important that cavity barriers that restrict the spread of fire are installed appropriately, especially to walls and floors that need to be fire-resisting. (This type of construction is unlikely to be found in many equine establishments.)

If you are in any doubt as to whether any remedial work will be required, then advice should be sought from a competent person.

Breaching fire separation

To ensure effective protection against fire and smoke, walls and floors providing fire separation must form a complete barrier, with an equivalent level of fire resistance provided to any openings such as doors, ventilation ducts, pipe and wire passages or refuse chutes.

The passing of services such as heating pipes, telephone or electrical cables through fire-resisting partitions leaves gaps through which fire and smoke will rapidly spread. This should be rectified by suitable fire-stopping and there are many proprietary products available to suit particular types of construction. Competent contractors should install such products.[10]

Decor and surface finishes of walls, ceilings and escape routes

The materials used to line walls and ceilings can contribute significantly to the spread of flame across their surface. Most materials that are used as surface linings will fall into one of three classes of surface spread of flame. The following are common examples of acceptable materials for various situations:

Class 0: Materials suitable for circulation spaces and escape routes

Such materials include brickwork, blockwork, concrete, ceramic tiles, plaster finishes (including rendering on wood or metal lathes), wood-wool cement slabs and mineral fibre tiles or sheets with cement or resin binding.

Note: Additional finishes to these surfaces may be detrimental to the fire performance of the surface. If there is any doubt about this then the manufacturer of the finish should be consulted.

Class 1: Materials suitable for use in all rooms but not on fire escape routes

Such materials include all the Class 0 materials referred to above. Additionally, timber, hardboard, blockboard, particle board, heavy flock wallpapers and thermosetting plastics will be suitable if flame-retardant treated to achieve a Class 1 standard.

Class 3: Materials suitable for use in rooms of less than 30m²

Such materials include all those referred to in Class 1, including those that have not been flame-retardant treated and certain dense timber or plywood and standard glass-reinforced polyesters.

Decorations and display materials

You should evaluate what material could ignite first and what would cause the fire to develop and spread, and assess how materials used in temporary or permanent displays would interact with surface linings and position them accordingly. In particular, displays such as paper, textiles, festive decorations and trees or other flimsy materials should not be located in stairways or corridors. However, such materials may be acceptable in other locations if treated with an appropriate fire-retardant product.

Staff and visitor information boards should be confined to appropriately located display areas away from internal escape routes. Display boards should not be located in animal accommodation areas or placed on escape routes unless they are no bigger than 1m² or have been enclosed in a sealed display case cover.

---

[10] See advice on third party certification in Appendix E: References.

Appropriate standards

Further details about internal linings are available in Approved Document B, Appendix A. Appropriate testing procedures are detailed in BS 476 and, where appropriate, BS EN 13501.

The Building Research Establishment has published further guidance on types of fire-resisting construction (see Appendix E: Glossary).

C2 Fire-resisting doors

Requirements of a fire-resisting door

Effective fire-resisting doors, including any compartmentation of large, open-plan floor areas in animal premises, are vital to ensure that the occupants of buildings can evacuate to a place of safety. Correctly specified and well-fitted doors will hold back fire and smoke, preventing escape routes becoming unusable and total smoke logging of open stable floor areas, as well as preventing the fire spreading from one stable area to another.

Fire-resisting doors are necessary in any doorway located in a fire-resisting structure. Most internal doors are constructed of timber. These will give some limited protection against fire spread, but only a purpose-built fire-resisting door that has been tested to an approved standard will provide the necessary protection. Metal fire-resisting doors are also available and specific guidance for these is provided below.

All fire-resisting doors are rated by their performance when tested to an appropriate standard. The level of protection provided by the door is measured primarily by determining the time taken for a fire to breach the integrity (E) of the door assembly, together with its resistance to the passage of hot gases and flame.

Timber fire-resisting doors require a gap of 2–4mm between the door leaf and the frame. Installing an intumescent seal, in either the door or, preferably, the frame, normally protects this gap. This seal expands in the early stages of a fire and enhances the protection given by the door. In nearly all cases, additional smoke seals will be required to prevent the spread of smoke at ambient temperatures. Doors fitted with smoke seals have their classification code suffixed with a 'Sa'.

Note: Fire-resisting doors positioned in areas where animals are located should be suitably protected against damage from animals kicking or biting them.

The principal fire-resisting door categories are:

- E20 fire-resisting door providing 20 minutes fire resistance (or equivalent FD 20S) (note: many suppliers no longer provide an E20-type fire-resisting door);

- E30 fire-resisting door providing 30 minutes fire resistance (or equivalent FD 30S); and

- E60 fire-resisting door providing 60 minutes fire resistance (or equivalent FD 60S).

Fire-resisting doors are available that will provide up to 120 minutes fire resistance but their use is limited to more specialised conditions that are beyond the scope of this guidance.

Metal fire-resisting doors

Although the majority of fire-resisting doors are made from timber, metal fire-resisting doors, which meet the appropriate standard, can often be used for the same purpose. However, there are situations, especially in large retail premises, where they are more appropriate. The majority of metal fire-resisting door manufacturers will specify bespoke frames and hardware for their door sets.

For detailed guidance refer to Approved Document B.

Fire-resisting door furniture

Hinges

To ensure compliance with their rated fire performance, fire-resisting doors must be hung with the correct number, size and quality of hinges. Normally a minimum of three hinges is required; however, the manufacturer's instructions should be closely followed. BS EN 1935, including Annex B, is the appropriate standard.

Self-closing devices

All fire-resisting doors, other than those to locked cupboards and service ducts, should be fitted with an approved controlled self-closing device that will effectively close the door from any angle. In certain circumstances, concealed, jamb-mounted closing devices may be

---

[11] Further information can be obtained from the Door and Shutter Manufacturers Association (DSMA).

specified and in these cases should be capable of closing the door from any angle and against any latch fitted to the door; spring hinges are unlikely to be suitable. All self-closing devices should comply with BS EN 1154.

Electrically operated hold-open devices

In situations such as corridors used by large numbers of people or when mobility-impaired people may have difficulty in opening fire doors, electrically operated devices that hold the fire door open until it is automatically closed in a fire situation may be fitted.

Typical examples of such devices include:

- electro-magnetic devices fitted to the fire-resisting door and the adjacent wall which release when the electrically operated fire alarm operates;

- electro-magnetic devices located within the self-closing device; and

- 'free swing' self-closing devices, which operate by allowing the fire door leaf to work independently of the closing device in normal conditions. An electro-magnetic device within the self-closer linked to the fire alarm system ensures that the door closes on the operation of the fire alarm.

Other devices which perform the same function are available and may be acceptable.

With these systems, the device is activated either by an electrical fire alarm system incorporating automatic smoke detectors or by independent smoke detectors (not domestic smoke alarms) on each side of the door, installed solely for that purpose.

In all cases, the door should close when the fire alarm is operated or in the event of a power failure. Where such devices are used it should be possible to close the door manually.

The advice of a fire safety expert should be sought before hold-open devices are installed. Such devices should, where appropriate, comply with BS EN 1155.

Glazing in fire-resisting doors

Although glazing provides additional safety in everyday use and can enhance the appearance of fire-resisting doors, it should never reduce the fire resistance of the door. The opening provided in the door for the fire-resisting glazing unit(s) and the fitting of the beading are critical, and should only be entrusted to a competent person. In nearly all cases the door and glazing should be purchased from a reputable supplier who can provide documentary evidence that the door continues to achieve the required rating.

Glazing in fire-resisting doors should never be permitted where animals are present, other than small observation panels for people to see if there is anyone on the other side of the door.

Door signs

Fire-resisting doors that have been fitted with self-closing devices should be labelled 'Fire door keep shut'. Fire doors to cupboards, stores and service ducts that are not self-closing because they are routinely kept locked should be labelled 'Fire door keep locked'. All signs should comply with BS 5499-5.

Installation and workmanship

The reliability and performance of correctly specified fire-resisting doors can be undermined by inadequate installation. It is important that installers with the necessary level of skill and knowledge are used. Accreditation schemes for installers of fire-resisting doors are available.[12]

Maintenance of fire doors

Timber fire-resisting doors will need to be regularly checked to ensure they are in good working order. Inspect doors for any damage, warping or distortion that will hinder the door from closing flush into the frame.

- Ensure that self-closing devices operate effectively and any hold-open devices release upon activation of the fire alarm.

- Check that any fire-resisting glazed panels are in good condition and secure in their frame.

- Check that intumescent strips and smoke-stopping seals are in good condition.

- Check door signs to ensure they are present and legible.

[12] See third party certification in Appendix E: References.

Figure 57: A fire-resisting and smoke stopping door

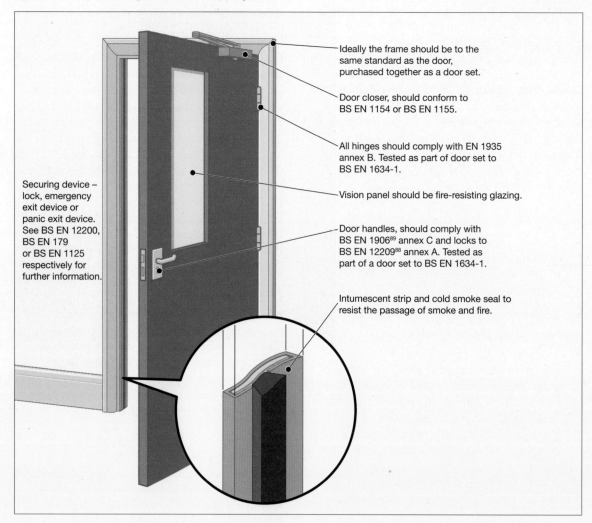

Securing device – lock, emergency exit device or panic exit device. See BS EN 12200, BS EN 179 or BS EN 1125 respectively for further information.

Ideally the frame should be to the same standard as the door, purchased together as a door set.

Door closer, should conform to BS EN 1154 or BS EN 1155.

All hinges should comply with EN 1935 annex B. Tested as part of door set to BS EN 1634-1.

Vision panel should be fire-resisting glazing.

Door handles, should comply with BS EN 1906[89] annex C and locks to BS EN 12209[88] annex A. Tested as part of a door set to BS EN 1634-1.

Intumescent strip and cold smoke seal to resist the passage of smoke and fire.

Other types of fire doors and shutters will require routine maintenance, particularly of the power operation and release and closing mechanisms.

Further information is available on fire doors in BS 8214. If you are unsure about the quality, effectiveness or fitting of your fire doors, you should consult a fire safety expert.

C3 Door-fastening devices

The relationship between the securing of doors against unwanted entry and the ability to escape through them easily in an emergency has often proved problematical. Careful planning and the use of quality materials remain the most effective means of satisfying both of these objectives.

Any device that impedes people making good their escape, either by being unnecessarily complicated to manipulate or not being readily openable, will not be acceptable.

External fastenings on fire exit doors that also serve as emergency access points into the building to reach the stalls to release the horses in an emergency will need to be carefully thought through so as not to create any security problems.

Where large or long stable buildings are provided with a fire exit door at each end and positioned mid-way along the length of the building, these fire exit doors may also have to serve as emergency access doors for people attempting to enter and release the animals when the building has been locked at the end of the working day and is unattended.

Guidance on fire exit doors starts from the position that exit doors on escape routes should not normally be fitted with **any** locking devices (electrically operated or otherwise), but accepts that in many cases the need for security will require some form of device that prevents unlimited access but still enables the occupants of a building or area to open the door easily should a fire occur. These devices can take many forms, but, in the majority of cases, premises where visitors, livery owners, members of the public or others who are not familiar with the building are present should use panic bar devices conforming to BS EN 1125 (i.e. push bars or touch bars).[13] External access devices may also be fitted to the devices to provide access to authorised personnel for routine or emergency purposes.

Premises that have limited numbers of employees or others who are familiar with the building and where panic is not likely may use devices conforming to BS EN 179 (i.e. push pads or lever handles).[14]

Electromechanical devices

The development of entry control devices, based on electromechanical lock keeps and draw bolts, which can be controlled by people inside the premises by entering some form of code or by using 'smart cards', has been adapted to also control the exit from certain areas. These devices have been fitted in many non-animal premises and may be linked to the fire detection and/or warning system. Experience has indicated that these devices can fail to open in a number of ways. They are dependent on a spring mechanism to return the lock keep or draw bolt(s) and are liable to jam when pressure is applied to the door. It is also relatively easy to fit them incorrectly. Electromechanical locking devices **are normally unacceptable on escape doors**, unless it can be verified that they do not rely on a spring mechanism, fail-safe open and are not affected by pressure, in which case the criteria for electromagnetic devices must be adhered to (see conditions below).

Electromagnetic devices

These are generally considered to be more reliable due to the absence of moving parts and their inherent 'fail-safe' operation. Electromagnetic locking devices go some way to addressing the particular concerns surrounding electromechanical locking systems. The release of this type of device is controlled

by the interruption of electrical current to an electromagnet, either manually via a break-glass point (typically coloured green) or by linking to the premises' fire warning and/or detection system.

Again, break-glass arrangements should not be considered in premises where animals are housed.

Time-delay devices on escape routes

A further development is the fitting of a time-delay system to the electronic door-locking device. This delays the actual opening of an exit door for a variable period following operation of the panic bar or other exit device. Periods of between five and 60 seconds can be pre-set at the manufacturing stage or can be adjusted when fitted.

These arrangements are not usually acceptable for use by members of the public. However, they may be acceptable for use by staff who are familiar with their operation and are suitably trained in their use.

Management of electronic door-control devices including time delays

Enforcing authorities may accept the use of such devices, if the responsible person can demonstrate through a suitable fire risk assessment for each individual door both the need and the adequate management controls to ensure that people can escape safely and animals can be released quickly and easily from the premises. In particular:

- Access control should not be confused with exit control. Many devices are available which control access to the premises but retain the immediate escape facility from the premises.

- In areas used by the public or visitors, when push bars are operated on escape doors they should release the electromagnetic locks immediately and allow the exit doors to open.

- The requirement for exit control should be carefully assessed and should not be seen as a substitute for good management of the staff and other occupants.

[13] BS EN 1125: *Building hardware. Panic exit devices operated by a horizontal bar. Requirements and test methods*, British Standards Institution, 1997.
[14] BS EN 179: *Building hardware. Emergency exit devices operated by a lever handle or push pad. Requirements and test methods*, British Standards Institution, 1998.

- The use of electronic door-locking devices should be considered with particular care in premises with a number of different occupancies. The management of a complicated system of evacuation for many different groups of people is unlikely to be practicable.

- The technical standards in respect of sourcing, maintaining and testing must be of the highest order.

- When part of the management control system involves trained personnel assisting others at these doors, the availability of these personnel must be rigorously controlled

- The use of exit control devices should not be considered where the number of trained personnel is low and members of the public would be expected to operate the devices without assistance. Their use in places of assembly should not be considered without the highest degree of supervision and control.

- In premises where there may be large numbers of people, the devices should only be considered when linked to a comprehensive automatic fire detection and warning system in accordance with BS 5839. There should be an additional means of manually overriding the locking device at each such exit (typically a green break-glass point, but not in areas occupied by animals).

- The use of time-delay systems that prevent the opening of emergency exits for a pre-set time are primarily used to improve security. These add a further layer of complexity to the fire strategy and **should not be considered in public areas** and on exits used for the release of animals. They should only be used in non-public areas when all other options, such as relocating valuable stock or exterior boundary management, have been addressed. Their value in preventing theft is likely to be transient, as the use of the manual override becomes more widely known.

BS 8220[15] gives further advice on security in buildings, and while this standard does refer to electronic locking devices it also acknowledges that the balance must remain on the side of emergency escape rather than security.

[15] BS 8220: *Guide for security of buildings against crime*, British Standards Institution.

Appendix D

Historic animal buildings and stables

General considerations

In addition to the guidance about the 'five-step' fire risk assessment elsewhere in this guide, this appendix offers additional information about listed and historical animal buildings.

Fire risk assessments conducted for all animal establishments which are listed as historic buildings, or part of a historic building, will need to ensure that a balance is struck between ensuring sufficient fire safety measures are in place for the safety of people, and avoiding extensive alterations to help maintain the character of the building. Advice will also have to be sought for improving the safety and release of the animals.

In addition to the fire risk assessment, it is recommended that a general fire policy statement and manual be compiled. A person must be nominated to take responsibility for all aspects of fire safety. Usually the person charged with the management and control of the premises will be the responsible person under the Regulatory Reform (Fire Safety) Order 2005.

The advice and/or consent of the local building control authority should form part of any fire risk assessment that impacts on the character of the building (e.g. replacement or additional doors, openings, fittings, wooden panelling and decor) or material changes to existing escape routes. An ideal solution is one that is reversible, enabling the historic elements to be reinstated.

A fire safety adviser will be able to suggest alternatives to conventional fire precautions, such as:

- a fire engineering solution;

- upgrading existing doors and partitions in a sympathetic manner to improve their fire resistance; and

- considering the installation of specialist fire detection or suppression systems.

Should the design and nature of the historic building preclude the introduction of conventional fire safety features, it will be necessary to use and manage the building in such a way that:

- limits the number of occupants, either staff, visitors or members of the public (or animals) inside the building(s);

- limits activities in the building; and

- provides adequate supervision within the building.

In stable buildings that are open to the public, you may wish to designate parts as 'off limits' to the general public. The locking of internal doors and the use of fixed or movable barriers should not restrict the availability of alternative escape routes.

Liaison with the fire and rescue service

The responsible person will need to ensure effective liaison with the fire and rescue service to enable them to carry out effective firefighting operations. This may include information on:

- the provision of emergency water supplies and any associated pumps (particular attention should be paid to sources that may dry up in the summer months, e.g. seasonal ponds, lakes and underground tanks);

- difficult access for firefighting vehicles;

- particular hazards in the construction features of the building;

- the use of combustible under-floor insulation;

- underground vaults, ducts and voids where fire may spread unchecked;

- worn stone slabs in staircase construction; and

- the presence of cast iron columns and wrought iron beams in the building's construction.

Emergency planning

An important consideration for the proprietors, owners and trustees of equine premises is the protection of valuable artefacts and structural features from the effects of fire. However, the efficient evacuation of all occupants, including the animals, must take precedence over procedures for limiting damage to property and contents. Salvage work or damage limitation should be limited to those parts of the buildings not directly affected by the fire.

Fire wardens and other members of staff tasked with carrying out salvage work should have received formal training and adequate protective clothing and be fully briefed about the health and safety risk assessment carried out to identify the dangers associated with this activity. Further detailed advice on fire safety in historic buildings can found in the following publications:

- BS 7913: Guide to the principles of the conservation of historic buildings, British Standards Institution, 1988

- Heritage under fire: A guide to the protection of historic buildings, Fire Protection Association (for the UK Working Party on Fire Safety in Historic Buildings), 1991, ISBN 0 902167 94 4

- The Installation of Sprinkler Systems in Historic Buildings (Historic Scotland Technical Advice Note 14), Fire Protection Association (TCRE Division/Scottish Conservation Bureau, Hist.), 1998, ISBN 1 900168 63 4

- Fire Protection Measures in Scottish Historic Buildings: Advice on Measures Required to Minimise the Likelihood of Fire Starting and to Alleviate the Destructive Consequences of Fire in Historic Buildings (Technical Advice Note 11), TCRE Division/Scottish Conservation Bureau, Hist., 1997, ISBN 1 900168 41 3

- Fire Risk Management in Heritage Buildings (Technical Advice Note 22), TCRE Division/Scottish Conservation Bureau, Hist., 2001, ISBN 1 900168 71 5

- Summary and conclusions of the report into fire protection measures for the Royal Palaces by Sir Alan Bailey following the Windsor Castle fire, 1992

- The fire at Upton Park, National Trust

- Timber panelled doors and fire, English Heritage

- Fire safety in historic town centres, English Heritage and Cheshire Fire and Rescue Service

Appendix E
Glossary and references

Glossary of terms

These definitions are provided to assist the responsible person in understanding some of the technical terms used in this guide. They are not exhaustive and more precise definitions may be available in other guidance.

Term	Definition
Access area	An area through which passes the only escape route from an inner room or area.
Access room	A room through which passes the only escape route from an inner room.
Accommodation stairway	A stairway, additional to that required for means of escape purposes, provided for the convenience of occupants.
Alternative escape route	Escape routes sufficiently separated by either direction and space, or by fire-resisting construction, to ensure that one is still available irrespective of the location of a fire.
Approved Document B (ADB)	Guidance issued by government in support of the fire safety aspects of the building regulations.
Automatic fire detection system	A means of automatically detecting the products of a fire and sending a signal to a fire warning system. The design and installation should conform to BS 5839. See 'Fire warning'.
Automatic fire suppression system	A means of automatically suppressing, controlling or extinguishing a fire.
Automatic release mechanism	A device that will automatically release either a locking mechanism on an exit route or a hold-open device to a door or roller shutter. It should operate manually, on actuation of the fire warning or detection system or on failure of the power supply.
Automatic self-closing device	A device that is capable of closing the door from any angle and against any latch fitted to the door.
Basement	A storey with a floor which at some point is more than 1,200mm below the highest level of ground adjacent to the outside walls, unless, and for escape purposes only, such an area has adequate, independent and separate means of escape.
Child	A person who is not over compulsory school age, construed in accordance with the Education Act 1996.
Class 0 surface spread of flame	Class 0 materials not only restrict the rate of surface spread of flame but also the rate at which heat is released from them. Class 0 is a higher standard than those referred to in British Standards.
Compartment wall and/or floor	A fire-resisting wall or floor that separates one fire compartment from another.
Competent person	A person with sufficient training and experience or knowledge and other qualities to enable him/her properly to assist in undertaking the preventive and protective measures.

Term	Definition
Dead end	Area from which escape is possible in one direction only.
Direct distance	The shortest distance from any point within the floor area to the nearest storey exit, or fire-resisting route, ignoring walls, partitions and fixings.
Domestic premises	Premises occupied as a private dwelling, excluding those areas used in common by the occupants of more than one such dwelling.
Emergency lighting	Lighting provided for use when the supply to the normal lighting fails.
Enforcing authority	The fire and rescue authority or any other authority specified in Article 25 of the Regulatory Reform (Fire Safety) Order 2005.
Escape lighting	That part of the lighting system provided to enable people to use the escape route (it may be the normal lighting system).
Escape route	Route forming that part of the means of escape from any point in a building to a final exit.
Evacuation lift	A lift that may be used for the evacuation of people with disabilities, or others, in a fire.
External escape stair	Stair providing an escape route, external to the building.
False alarm	A fire signal, usually from a fire warning system, resulting from a cause other than fire.
Final exit	An exit from a building where people can continue to disperse in safety and where they are no longer in danger from fire and/or smoke.
Fire compartment	A building, or part of a building, constructed to prevent the spread of fire to or from another part of the same building or an adjoining building.
Fire door	A door or shutter, together with its frame and furniture, provided for the passage of people, air or goods which, when closed, is intended to restrict the passage of fire and/or smoke to a predictable level of performance.
Fire exit securing device	An appropriate device for securing a fire exit, which allows a person to easily and immediately open that fire exit in an emergency. Any device that requires a key or is overly complicated will be unacceptable.
Firefighting lift	A lift, designed to have additional protection, with controls that enable it to be used under the direct control of the fire and rescue service when fighting a fire.
Firefighting shaft	A fire-resisting enclosure containing a firefighting stair, fire mains, firefighting lobbies and, if provided, a firefighting lift.
Firefighting stair	See firefighting shaft.

Term	Definition
Fire resistance	The ability of a component or construction of a building to satisfy, for a stated period of time, some or all of the appropriate criteria of BS EN 1363-1, BS 476-7 and associated standards. (Generally described as 30 minutes fire-resisting or 60 minutes fire-resisting.)
Fire safety manager	A nominated person with responsibility for carrying out day-to-day management of fire safety. (This may or may not be the same as the 'responsible person'.)
Fire safety strategy	A number of planned and co-ordinated arrangements designed to reduce the risk of fire and to ensure safety of people in the event of fire.
Fire-stopping	A seal provided to close an imperfection of fit or design tolerance between elements or components, to restrict the passage of fire and smoke.
Fire warning system	A means of alerting people to the existence of a fire. (See automatic fire detection system.)
Highly flammable	Generally liquids with a flashpoint of below 21°C. (The Chemicals (Hazard Information and Packaging for Supply) Regulations 2002 (CHIP) give more detailed guidance.)
Inner room	A room from which escape is possible only by passing through another room (the access room).
Licensed premises	Any premises that require a licence under any statute to undertake trade or conduct business activities.
Maintained lighting	Emergency lighting that is kept illuminated at all relevant times.
Material change	An alteration to a building, process or service which significantly affects the level of risk in that building.
Means of escape	Route(s) provided to ensure safe egress from premises or other locations to a place of total safety, including the release of both personnel and animals from the buildings.
Monitoring station	An organisation which accepts alarm signals from premises and carries out a pre-determined response.
Non-maintained lighting	Emergency lighting that illuminates only on failure of the normal supply.
Occupancy density factor	A means of estimating the occupant capacity of a particular room or space in a building, based on an assumption of a certain number of m² for each person.
Occupancy profile	The physiological and psychological characteristics of the individuals who may reasonably be expected to use the building.
Phased evacuation	A system of evacuation in which different parts of the premises are evacuated in a controlled sequence of phases, those parts of the premises expected to be at greatest risk being evacuated first.
Place of total safety	A place, away from the building, in which people are at no immediate danger from the effects of a fire.

Term	Definition
Place of total safety for animals	An emergency enclosure, preferably upwind from the fire, where animals can be taken and are at no immediate danger from the effects of a fire.
Premises	Any place, such as a building and the immediate land bounded by any enclosure of it, any tent, moveable or temporary structure or any installation or workplace.
Progressive horizontal evacuation	An escape strategy that allows for the horizontal movement of people, from one fire compartment to another, away from the fire.
Protected lobby	A fire-resisting enclosure providing access to an escape stairway via two sets of fire-resisting doors and into which no room opens other than toilets and lifts.
Protected stairway	A stairway which is adequately protected from the rest of the building by fire-resisting construction.
Reasonable safety	A place within a building or structure where, for a limited period of time, people will have some protection from the effects of fire and smoke. This place, usually a corridor or stairway, will normally have a minimum of 30 minutes fire resistance and allow people to continue their escape to a place of total safety.
Refuge	An area of reasonable safety in which a disabled person may rest prior to reaching a place of total safety. It should lead directly to a fire-resisting escape route.
Responsible person	The person ultimately responsible for fire safety as defined in the Regulatory Reform (Fire Safety) Order 2005.
Significant finding	A feature of the premises, its contents or occupants that may have an adverse effect on the means of escape in case of fire, resulting in a potential risk to people within or in the vicinity of the premises.
Simultaneous evacuation	A system of evacuation in which all people evacuate immediately on hearing the fire warning.
Smoke alarm	Device containing within one housing all the components, except possibly the energy source, for detecting smoke and giving an audible alarm.
Staged alarm	A fire warning system which can produce a number of staged alarms within a given area.
Storey exit	An exit giving direct access into a fire-resisting stairway or an external escape route.
Travel distance	The actual distance to be travelled by a person from any point within the floor area to the nearest storey exit or final exit, having regard to the layout of walls, partitions and fixings.
Vision panel	A transparent panel in a wall or door of an inner room enabling the occupant to become aware of a fire in the access area during the early stages.

References

British Standard EN 1154	Building hardware. Controlled door-closing devices. Requirements and test methods.
British Standard EN 1935	Building hardware. Single-axis hinges. Requirements and test methods.
British Standard EN 1634-1	Fire resistance tests for door and shutter assemblies. Part 1: Fire doors and shutters.
British Standard 476-22	Fire tests on building materials and structures. Methods for the determination of the fire resistance of non-load-bearing elements of construction.
British Standard PD 6512-3	Use of elements of structural fire protection with particular reference to the recommendations given in BS 5588 Fire precautions in the design and construction of buildings. Part 3: Guide to the fire performance of glass.
British Standard 8300	The design of buildings and their approaches to meet the needs of disabled people. Code of practice.
British Standard 5588-8	Fire precautions in the design, construction and use of buildings. Code of practice for means of escape for disabled people.
British Standard 5588-10	Fire precautions in the design, construction and use of buildings. Code of practice for shopping complexes.
British Standard 5395-3	Stairs, ladders and walkways. Code of practice for the design of industrial type stairs, permanent ladders and walkways.
British Standard 5588-11	Fire precautions in the design, construction and use of buildings. Code of practice for shops, offices, industrial, storage and other similar buildings.
British Standard EN 81	Safety rules for the construction and installation of lifts.
British Standard EN 81-70	Safety rules for the construction and installation of lifts. Particular applications for passenger and goods passenger lifts. Accessibility to lifts for persons including persons with disability.
British Standard 5839-1	Fire detection and alarm systems for buildings. Code of practice for system design, installation, commissioning and maintenance.
British Standard 5839-6	Code of practice for the design and installation of fire detection and alarm systems in dwellings.
British Standard EN 54-5	Fire detection and fire alarm systems. Heat detectors. Point detectors.
British Standard EN 54-7	Fire detection and fire alarm systems. Smoke detectors. Point detectors using scattered light, transmitted light or ionisation.
British Standard EN 54-11	Fire detection and fire alarm systems. Manual call points.

British Standard EN 3-1	Portable fire extinguishers. Description, duration of operation, class A and B fire test.
British Standard 5041-1	Fire hydrant systems equipment. Specification for landing valves for wet risers.
British Standard 5041-2	Fire hydrant systems equipment. Specification for landing valves for dry risers.
British Standard 5041-3	Fire hydrant systems equipment. Specification for inlet breechings for dry riser inlets.
British Standard 5041-4	Fire hydrant systems equipment. Specification for boxes for landing valves for dry risers.
British Standard 5041-5	Fire hydrant systems equipment. Specification for boxes for foam inlets and dry riser inlets.
British Standard 5306-2 (plus LPC Technical Bulletins)	Fire extinguishing installations and equipment on premises. Specification for sprinkler systems.
British Standard 5306-1	Fire extinguishing installations and equipment on premises. Part 1: Hose reels and foam inlets.
British Standard EN 671-1	Fixed firefighting systems. Hose systems. Hose reels with semi-rigid hose.
British Standard EN 671-3	Fixed firefighting systems. Hose systems. Maintenance of hose reels with semi-rigid hose and hose systems with lay-flat hose.
British Standard 5306-3	Fire extinguishing installations and equipment on premises. Code of practice for the inspection and maintenance of portable fire extinguishers.
British Standard 5306-8	Fire extinguishing installations and equipment on premises. Selection and installation of portable fire extinguishers. Code of practice.
British Standard 7944	Type 1 heavy duty fire blankets and type 2 heavy duty heat protective blankets.
British Standard EN 1869	Fire blankets.
British Standard ISO 14520-1	Gaseous fire-extinguishing systems. Physical properties and system design. General requirements.
British Standard 5266-1	Emergency lighting. Code of practice for the emergency lighting of premises other than cinemas and certain other specified premises used for entertainment.
British Standard 5266-2	Emergency lighting. Code of practice for electrical low mounted way guidance systems for emergency use.
British Standard 5266-6	Emergency lighting. Code of practice for non-electrical low mounted way guidance systems for emergency use. Photoluminescent systems.
British Standard EN 1838	Lighting applications. Emergency lighting.
British Standard EN 60598-1	Luminaires. General requirements and tests.

British Standard 5499-4	Safety signs, including fire safety signs. Code of practice for escape route signing.
British Standard 5499-1	Graphical symbols and signs. Safety signs, including fire safety signs. Specification for geometric shapes, colours and layout.
British Standard 9990	Code of practice for non-automatic firefighting systems in buildings.
British Standard 476-7	Fire tests on building materials and structures. Method of test to determine the classification of the surface spread of flame of products.
British Standard EN 13501-1	Fire classification of construction products and building elements. Classification using test data from reaction to fire tests.
British Standard EN 1634-1	Fire resistance tests for door and shutter assemblies. Fire doors and shutters.
British Standard EN 1634-3	Fire resistance tests for door and shutter assemblies. Smoke control doors and shutters.
British Standard 8214	Code of practice for fire door assemblies with non-metallic leaves.
Proposed British Standard pr EN 14637	Building hardware. Electrically controlled hold-open systems for fire/smoke door assemblies. Requirements, test methods, application and maintenance. (Consultation document.)
British Standard EN 1125	Building hardware. Panic exit devices operated by a horizontal bar. Requirements and test methods.
British Standard EN 179	Building hardware. Emergency exit devices operated by a lever handle or push pad. Requirements and test methods.
British Standard 8220-21995	Guide for security of buildings against crime. Offices and shops.
British Standard EN 45020	Standardisation and related activities. General vocabulary.
British Standard 5588-5	Fire precautions in the design, construction and use of buildings. Code of practice for firefighting stairs and lifts.
ISO 13784-2	Reaction to fire tests for sandwich panel building systems. Part 2: Test method for large rooms.
British Standard 6661	Guide for the design, construction and maintenance of single-skin air supported structures.
British Standard 5268-4.2	Structural use of timber. Fire resistance of timber structures. Recommendations for calculating fire resistance of timber stud walls and joisted floor constructions.
Building Research Establishment Report BR 128	Guidelines for the construction of fire-resisting structural elements.

Successful health and safety management, HSG 65, second edition. HSE Books, 2000. ISBN 0 7176 1276 7.

Guide to fire precautions in existing places of work that require a fire certificate. Factories, offices, shops and railway premises. HMSO. ISBN 0 11 341079 4.

Design principles of fire safety. HMSO, 1996. ISBN 0 11 753045 X.

Chemicals (Hazard Information and Packaging for Supply) Regulations 2002 and supporting guides.

Health and Safety (Signs and Signals) Regulations 1996.

The approved supply list, seventh edition, and *The approved classification and labelling guide,* 2002.

Dangerous Substances and Explosive Atmospheres Regulations 2002. Approved code of practice and guidance. HSE Books, 2003. ISBN 0 7176 2203 7.

Maintaining portable electrical equipment in offices and other low-risk environments, INDG236. HSE Books, 1996. ISBN 0 7176 12724.

Guidance on the acceptance of electronic locks to doors required for means of escape. The Chief and Assistant Chief Fire Officers Association.

Ensuring best practice for passive fire protection in buildings. Building Research Establishment, 2003. ISBN 1 870409 19 1.

DCLG/CACFOA/BFPSA guidance on reducing false alarms.

Smoke shafts protecting fire shafts; their performance and design. BRE Report 79204. Building Research Establishment,:2002.

The Building Regulations 2000 Approved Document B fire safety. ISBN 0 85112 351 2.

The Building Regulations 2000 Approved Document B fire safety 2006 Volume 2, Appendix B, Table B1.

Design, construction, specification and fire management of insulated envelopes for temperature controlled environments. International Association for Cold Storage Construction.

The use of PTF-based material for tension-membrane roofs and structures, BRE Report 274. Building Research Establishment, 1994.

Safety signs and signals. The Health and Safety (Safety Signs and Signals) Regulations 1996. Guidance on regulations, L64. HSE Books, 1997. ISBN 0 7176 0870 0.

BS 7913: *The principles of the conservation of historic buildings.* British Standards Institution, 1988.

Heritage under fire: A guide to the protection of historic buildings. Fire Protection Association for the UK Working Party on Fire Safety in Historic Buildings, 1991. ISBN 0 902167 94 4.

The installation of sprinkler systems in historic buildings, TAN 14. ISBN 1 900168 63 4.

Fire protection measures in Scottish historic buildings, TAN 11. ISBN 1 900168 41 3.

Fire risk management in heritage buildings, TAN 22. ISBN 1 900168 71 5.

Fires and human behaviour, second edition. David Fulton Publishers, 2000. ISBN 1 85346 105 9.

Management of Health and Safety at Work Regulations 1999. Approved code of practice and guidance, L21. HSE Books, 2000. ISBN 0 7176 2488 9.

Further reading

Management of Health and Safety at Work Regulations 1999, SI 1999/3242.

Design principles of fire safety. The Stationery Office, 1996. ISBN 0 11 753045 X.

Chemicals (Hazard Information and Packaging for Supply) Regulations 2002, SI 2002/1689. The Stationery Office, 2002. ISBN 0 11 042419 0.

Supporting guides:
The idiot's guide to CHIP 3: Chemicals (Hazard Information and Packaging for Supply) Regulations, 2002, INDG350.

HSE Books, 2002. ISBN 0 7176 2333 5 (single copy free or priced packs of 5);

CHIP for everyone, HSG228. HSE Books, 2002. ISBN 0 7176 2370 X.

Guidance on the acceptance of electronic locks to doors required for means of escape. Published by The Chief and Assistant Chief Fire Officers' Association.

Ensuring best practice for passive fire protection in buildings. Building Research Establishment, 2003. ISBN 1 870409 19 1.

Smoke shafts protecting fire shafts: their performance and design, BRE Project Report 79204. Building Research Establishment, 2002.

Fire safety of PTFE-based material used in building, BRE Report 274. Building Research Establishment, 1994. ISBN 0 851256 53 8.

Fires and human behaviour. David Fulton Publishers, 2000. ISBN 1 85346 105 9.

Management of health and safety at work. Management of Health and Safety at Work Regulations 1999.

Approved code of practice and guidance, L21 (second edition). HSE Books, 2000. ISBN 0 7176 2488 9.

Guidelines for fire safety in equine and agricultural premises. Harry Paviour, The British Horse Society.

Index

Page numbers in *italics* refer to information in Figures or Tables.

Riding Establishments Act 1964 5, 105
rising mains 66, 67, 121
risk
  definition 10
  evaluating 10, 11, *12,* 16–18, 20–1, 42, 50, 55, 80, *110*
  people at risk 10, *12,* 15, 16–18, 35, 80, *110, 122*
  reducing 10, *12,* 20–33, 35, 38, 42, 80, 88–90, *110*
  residual risk 20–1
roll calls 114, 117
roller shutter doors 58, 67, 88, 120, 133
roof exits 87–8

S

scenery 53, 54
SCOLA (Second Consortium of Local Authorities) construction method 125
seating 21, 53, 56, 100
security 32, 48, 54–5, 114, 128
shafts, firefighting *see* lifts
shared use *see* multi-occupied buildings
short-term hiring or leasing 7
signs and notices 31, 32, 49, 62, 101, 104–6, 121, 127
  information and instruction *36,* 39, 67, 105–6, 112, 114
smoke
  control of 52, 54, 58, 66, 90, 120, *124, 126, 128*
  dangers of 17, 52, 90, 93
  reservoirs 54
  spread of 17–18, 21, 29, 50–1, 52–4, 70, 79
smoke detectors 50, 59, 70, 75, *77,* 136
smoking 13, 16, 19, 21, 47, 49, 115
sprinklers 21, 33, 42, 65–6, 72, 90, 116
stables 4
  emergency escape lighting 30, 101–2
  escape routes 26, 68–9, 85
  evaluating risk 10, 11, 15, 16–17, 20, 21, 28, 50, 55
  existing layout and construction 50–1
  fire sources 13, 14, 19, 50
  firefighting equipment 25, 61, 62, 64–5
  hiring and leasing 7
  historic buildings 131–2
  housekeeping 46
  record-keeping 34
  see also animal premises; equine premises
staff
  co-operation and co-ordination 39, 40, 107, 115
  fire detection and warning systems 22, 57, 58–9
  fire drills 41, 107, 108, 116–17, 121
  fire safety training 6, 28, 34, 36, 37, 39, 40–1, 68, 90, 107, 111, 115–17, 120, 121
  firefighting training 23, 35, 41, 62, 64, *110,* 115, 116

information and instruction 6, 26, 28, 35, 38–9, 40, 50, 105–6, 112, 113, 114
  roles in emergency 37, 38, 40, 104, 111, 113, 114, 115, 130
  security 54
  staff numbers 50, 68, 69, 111, 130, 131
  see also contractors
stairways
  accommodation stairways 80, 85, 86, 93, 98, 133
  basements 78, 93, 94, *95,* 96, 98, 133
  bypass routes 84
  emergency escape lighting 101
  external 85, *86, 87,* 88, 134
  hazards in 28, 51, 80, 85, 93, 94, 96, 98, 120, 131
  protected 25, 70, 72, 80, *81,* 82–3, 90, 93, 96, *97,* 98, 136
  spiral and helical 86
  width and capacity of 66, 85
storage 11, 19, 41, 46–8, 105, 114, 124–5
straw 46, 47, 51, 63, 68, 124

T

tack rooms 11, 69, 105, 124
  source of ignition 13, 49
telephones 31, 114
temporary structures 7, 50, 53
tents 53
torches 30, 32, 101
training
  fire safety 6, 28, 34, 36, 37, 39, 40–1, 68, 90, 107, 111, 115–17, 120, 121
  firefighting equipment 23, 35, 39, 41, 62, 64, *110,* 115, 116
  record-keeping 41, 43, 107, 108, 116, 117

V

vandalism 19
vehicles 14, 19, 47, 55, 56
ventilation systems 14, 42, 48, 49, 54, 58, 66, 72, 120
vets 11
  risk to 15, 26
vision panels 70, 127, *128,* 136
visitors
  evacuating 37, 41
  information and instruction 113, 114
  risk to 15, 35, 50
voids 51, 70, 124, 125, 131
volunteers
  co-operation and co-ordination 39
  escape routes 28
  fire risk assessment 15, 35
  fire safety training 41, 115
  information and instruction 28, 36, 38–9, 40, 115
  roles in emergency 38

W

walls
    fire-resisting 27, 29, 52–3, 70, *86,* 123, 125, 133
    insulated core panels 51–2
    lining materials 14, 19, 123, 125–6
    see also partitions
waste and packaging, combustible 13, 14, 16, 19, 46, 50, 54, 114
water fog systems 25, 33, 65–6, 72, 90, 116
water tanks 25, 65, 67, 120, 131
way-finding systems 30, 102
windows, fire-resisting 85, *86,* 87, 124, 127, *128*
    vision panels 70, 127, *128,* 136

Y

yards 30, 88, 102

Z

zoos 4, 113